ORGASMIC EXPULSION

aka Female Ejaculation

**THE ROAD OF GOALS
THAT LED ME TO CREATE
THE BIG SOAK
INSTRUCTIONAL DVD**

**HOW I GOT
www.thebigsoak.org
TOP RANKED
on GOOGLE**

A GOAL DRIVEN - Auto-Biography
by Eric Jackson

ORGASMIC EXPULSION
Copyright © 2012 by Eric Jackson and
A.D. Echo Publishing Trust

Cover Art by: Teddy Fine
Editing Assistance by: Susan McClintock
                            DeBorah Brooks
Reference: Non-Fiction, Sex Education, How To, Goal Setting, Female Ejaculation, The Big Soak Instructional DVD
http://www.thebigsoak.org
http://www.orgasmicexpulsion.com
ISBN:13: 978-0-9855602-8-7
Published By A.D Echo Publishing Trust
http://www.adechopublishing.com

Table of Contents

Dedication

The course of my life has brought me to writing and self-publishing this text. I would like to dedicate it to so many of those people in my life whom I have loved. At some point our path's crossed in life but only for a temporary period of time.

Some of them are the same people that caused much of the turmoil over the past six years. To Joe and Sandra Santoro thanks for harboring me for 7 months as a tenant; knowing I was avoiding probation after crossing 4 state lines without permission from my probation officer. I thank them for turning me in for my violation of probation, in an effort to wrongfully evict me and not pay me for my hundreds of hours of construction work and caregiving for their 95 year old mother/grandmother. Without their poor foresight and displaced anger, I would not have had the opportunity to be writing this text from jail. Next to Michele Boehm, I missed having you in my life and Howard Boehm whom without, jail would never have been a part of my world; I would likely have lost countless dollars in the pizza business and likely never would have produced The Big Soak Instructional DVD without them in my life.

Now for those who truly love me. Sonny and Suni my parents for their constant antagonizing support in my life, which has always driven me to accomplish the impossible with the use of goal setting and the passion they both nurtured in me.

My son Max, though he always thought privately that I was a bit bananas, thinking that this could work, he always backed my ideas. To my son Jake, I Love You but you were too young to be aware of this project as it progressed in time, but thanks for being my wonderful son. Have passion, good communication and veracity in whatever you do!

My dear friend AJ Allen and his clan of amazing friends, they have all been a part of, and tolerated, my constant conversation over the past four years. Tracie Vaughn, over the years has been a tremendous supporter of my crazy ideas and always my best sounding board and inspiration to me. Michael Louis, you continue to be a supporter, as well as playing devil's advocate, regarding my far-fetched ideas.

Anthony Johnson, my cellmate who handed me the book that changed my entire direction in becoming an author. La Mesha of Twin Oaks, who kept me grounded and laughing, after I got out of jail.

Dan Poynter and his books which help and direct anyone who chooses to set a goal to author and self-publish.

Thanks to all the individuals that contributed to the video press release and production. To my customers who purchased THE BIG SOAK over the years, you contributed to its improvement, with your feedback, Thank You All.

Those who are now working with me on the new 5 year goal of: Video Surveys on the G-Area, which started in April of 2012 that I hope to use someday as part of my Doctoral Thesis.

Beverly Whipple PhD for her willingness to discuss the topic of female ejaculation with me and debate my points as if I were a colleague, without her motivating drive to push me forward in 2009 and keep spreading the word I am not sure that the idea for this book would have popped into my head.

Thank You All and so many other who have tolerated this conversation I have been having since 2004!

Foreword

Eric Jackson does not have any problem pouring his heart out for the passion he has for informing the world the truths about squirting orgasms and that it is a natural process. Eric met me on his back patio because late one night he was smoking a cigarette and I could see the ember glowing in the dark. Needless to say I was up late and jonzing for a smoke myself so I went and introduced myself to my courtyard neighbor. Since that time in 2008 he has been one of my closest friends and constant mentor. Eric offers a unique philosophy on life, the readers of this book will be offered that unique perspective to perhaps enhance their own skills. We have both grown and developed over the years, but Eric has never stopped following his goals no matter what the roadblocks.

After watching his DVD which I bought just so he would stop asking me, *to be honest*; but the facts are I learned from it. His ability to break down the process of how the depths of a woman's vagina functions is enlightening at very least. I counted myself very sexually experienced at thirty years old but I only had a basic understanding how the G-Spot worked in a girl. After watching this man's DVD and plenty of practice, any girl I become intimate with has been able to benefit from his techniques. Just by talking to them about this DVD I watched on squirting orgasms opens the conversation. Then depending on the comfort level between us ejaculations may follow. But I know I can now control whether I take it to that level.

Eric was man enough to research this subject to share with all of us. What he has done with this book and his instructional video program has given an education to anyone that wants to learn factual information.

He is currently helping me in the development of PUNK ROCK DUCK a product that started with the creative use of Duct Tape to make wallets and purses and has now grown into a custom t-shirt company as well. His words of inspiration and focus on turning dreams into goals has helped me take PUNK ROCK DUCK to the next level and start working on a website for the company.

A. J. Allen, B.A. JWU

p.s.

Eric and I are using his video knowledge to produce a reality v-cast on YouTube. It will be called The AJ and Eric Show. We intend to take my musical passions and his book and self-promote in bars until we make enough money to never work for someone else ever again.

www.youtube.com/AJandEric

Introduction

I offer these philosophies to the reader for an expanded understanding of what setting and achieving a goal can do when it comes to delivering your dreams and desires for yourself and your life, from your mind into the realities of the world.

I emphasize goal setting within this text regarding life and business as well as in a sexual relationship through communication.

I am comfortable that many will criticize the single fact that I believe Female Ejaculation is a behavior that can be learned and understood by all that choose. Many of you will purchase the book and then the DVD. Woven in these pages are bits of information that will perhaps allow you and your partner to gain understanding of the female vagina. Some of us are better at learning with visual aids like my DVD, while others need the written word to capture the ideas behind the process of what I am teaching.

At this time I would like to request any of my readers that have feedback about this text or the DVD itself to feel free to contact me directly at the email address in the order form on the last pages of this book.

Good Luck and Good Sex, Be DRIVEN in anything you choose to do in your life; it can be done!

School is for tests – tests are daily life!

"In life we attend schools to be given quizzes, tests, and finals on the information we have learned and shared. - When we independently attend to life, we are given quizzes, tests and finals, then it is up to us if we learn from them and share the lessons!"

Eric Jackson © 1991 - First Published 2012

How Much of
Sex is in Our Head?

It cuts both ways when it comes to sexuality and the brain of women and men. The knife is sharp and yet flexible if we allow it. Allowing ones' mind and body to get the best – we must give ourselves permission to feel our best for that slice of intimate time. Free your mind of negatives and trust in the other side of the blade of pleasurable possibilities.

We all must understand that the sexual relationship you establish is the most important of all when it comes to lifelong fulfillment. It is an interaction that you will be limited to your choice of mate, in theory. The principal of a sexual relationship with only one mate is the basis for a monogamous relationship; when they are successful throughout history the couple is quite content, happy and prosperous.

Women are much more creatures of emotions and tender mental thinking. Men tend to be fixers', we want to identify the problem and get past it. We men often lose sight of these differences and use excuses that we can't understand what our women are thinking. The fact is most of the time they tell us exactly what they are thinking. It is often in words that we men do not understand, so taking it slowly and asking for better explanations may often be the key to understanding and quality communication. Last week a wise woman in Love Park Philadelphia while filming interviews promoting this book told me "once you invest in a mate it is not worth spending the time to learn a new one! You've got to learn your man, and men learn your woman!" The video is viewable @PhillySexChat on YouTube.

So often we are NOT educated on various situations we may encounter in life. SEX is surely one of those situations. Any conversations we have with parents only include pregnancy and the consequences surrounding sex and STD's. Most conversations we have with our friends offer little factual information that we can count on. So we often learn from our partners as we experiment with sexual situations. Many times we allow ourselves to be put in situations where we are truly uncomfortable. Not knowing how to handle it, or even communicate about what is going on.

Often one partner has had more experience than the other and this too causes problems.

When learning about sex in school only the basic information about STD's, pregnancy and birth control is provided. It is understandable that the 10th grade health teacher really doesn't want to get into what is right or wrong in a sexual relationship. Nor do they have permission from the administration to discuss the feelings that surround sexual relations. They stay very vague and that is part of the problem.

Vague is problematic because we expect education to be clear and specific. So we tend to believe what we are taught, and vague causes expectations of the feelings to be vague as well.

When we finally find a partner to be sexual with we often are not sure what to do. Now the obvious is insert the penis in the vagina. This seems to be what many young men think is the extent of good sex. They seem to only want to get themselves off and few give true thought to the girl in the situation. Mostly due to lack of the skills to communicate with their partner, and determine what makes the woman fell pleasure. This is the beginning of unfairness in the bedroom. Men also know that they ejaculate in most all situations as the completion of their sexual encounters either with themselves or with a partner.

Over the past few decades with the onset of the VCR and then Internet, pornography has given more sexual education to the masses than any other source. The problem here is that people watching this type of imagery really take it at face value, not realizing that in truth is it is scripted and cameras can cut and restart. Video of hour long sexual escapades are pasted together from footage taken over an entire afternoon of filming.

I can think back to being young and watching soap opera kisses and thinking that this is the way a real passionate kiss is given. To have the mouth offset to your partners. Not realizing that it is what is called stage kissing and there is no passion whatsoever in most all cases. When our minds see something that we interpret as real we often take on the traits of that image as our own, allowing these situations to mentor our actions in our own relations with regard to sex.

Women too are lead to believe things that are not really set in reality. Women are not sure what to feel, or how it best works to make themselves feel best. There is little conversation between women concerning what is the real thing versus what is hopeful and or pretend all together. Hearing so many conflicting ideas of what makes sex great. Seeing so many Internet videos where it is done for the camera not the feeling, and more often for the male to get off from watching the video rather than the woman. Very rarely are the actions in the videos instructional by way of accurate movements or positions, again it is for the camera, the best way to film the vagina and entry of the penis or fingers or tongue. I am most disappointed in Internet video when I see lesbian play and they are also performing for the camera, not the actual feeling. Fingers inserted in the wrong positions, tongues in places that have little nerve ending to receive quality sexual feelings, but good footage for the audience.

So one could see where much of the confusion comes into play, lack of quality education.

Sexual relations, like most other things in life, are about learned behaviors and feelings. It can be taught by expert teachers and learned by receptive students. Again, sex is a learned behavior! Many people that were molested sexually will never completely heal to move forward because what was imprinted on their brains was distressing and not pleasant. The same often happens with female ejaculation. The imprinting

16

on the brain is often confusion and misunderstanding. Women read magazines like Cosmo and the like which describe orgasms in so many different ways, but rarely the ejaculation type. This leaves women to be a bit lost in the realities how to feel and react to various levels of intimacy.

Sexual stimulation feels good, but the definition of good is subjective with each woman. Many have according to statistics never achieved orgasm. Most have faked an orgasm at some point. It is a mind game that is not healthy. The brain imprinting that is caused by these behaviors becomes something that must be undone at some point. One would hope communication in a quality relationship would be the cure to some of this prior imprinting but that is the rare case. The assistance of a quality therapist could also help to correct this type of imprinting. But we all realize that good therapy is also rare. The majority of the medical profession is still, even today in 2012, not clear on the science of the female orgasm, or even the process surrounding female ejaculation. Many of the experts in the field studying female ejaculation are hesitant to pigeonhole all women in the category of those who can ejaculate. So where do we go from here?

Professionals are offering inconsistent opinions. Even today on the train a 4th year medical student was sure that women do not have a prostate gland; PSA in female ejaculate would contradict his understanding.

Women in general seem to be searching out their own answers at this point in history. The Internet seems to be the forum where the answers are being hunted and often delivered. In recent years the Internet has much more accurate information than anywhere else.

Having the support of Q and A sites and other Internet forums allows women to anonymously communicate with others that support them in their hunt for answers. This simple level of support is sometimes all that is needed to open the eyes of a confused woman. Having the explanations that now exist with accuracy allows many women to relate their personal situations to those of other women.

Now men listen up! If you are looking for a woman to feel comfortable with you long term, you need to communicate! Talking about her sexual needs and desires is a must. For most men sex talk with their significant other is comprised of "Hun, um can we fool around tonight?" It seems to me that the least talked about thing in this world of ours is the quality of sex within the relationship. You men need to do whatever is needed open the channels of communication. This more than anything else is what will allow a strong and healthy long term relationship. The lack of sexual communication is a guarantee to cause stress in a relationship. In my opinion much of the divorce in our nation is due to the overall lack of communication within the marital bedroom. So often couples go with the flow without really understanding what their partner is looking for in the sexual relationship, this in itself causes daily stresses and often cause affairs and divorce.

If you are looking to form a quality relationship communication is the key. This means in all facets. Women and men both are creatures of behaviors that are learned. What is in our heads is what governs our actions. When we talk to each other and do so with love and caring we tend to emerge stronger, this is true in almost all relationships.

Much of the reason that I have learned what I know is because of mistakes made within relationships I have had. The easiest way to hurt a woman is to not listen to her needs, in the case of sexual relationships even more so.

My intent with my DVD was to open lines of communication and perhaps save a relationship here and there. Surely my intent was to prevent a relationship from ending because of misunderstanding of the female ejaculating orgasm. There is no excuse in this day and age to be so misinformed that a man shuns a woman for what should by now be understood by all. Since 1980 the word has been out in the mass media. Since 2008 the word has been out all over the

Internet. I am hoping this book gets the conversation of female ejaculation back into the main stream media via TV, radio and cable news.

Words and understanding are the keys to the quality relationship. Work at what is important. Put in the time to get into the head of your woman. She likely was never given clear understanding of what was required to truly have a fulfilling sexual relationship. And for sure, if you are reading this text and watching the Instructional DVD you are on your way to improving the situation in your own life.

Consider an exercise in educating your partner on your personal likes and dislikes in the bedroom. This is not intended to make your partner feel any lacking; it is an exercise in understanding. Make a list of what turns you on in the bedroom. What feels nice and what does not really impact your pleasurable feelings. Each week share one of the likes and dislikes. Make an effort to attempt to not be judgmental and accommodate this special feeling for the person you

love.   It will build the ability to communicate and
expand your mutual pleasure and satisfaction.

<u>Words to live by!</u>

In life we are given two choices.
To be governed by Love or by Fear.
Love sees greatness in all things.
Fear discriminates and separates always!
Love allows us to enjoy the now!
Fear causes us to live in the past,
and clouds the present.
Love allows us to express ourselves openly.
Love allows pain to subside.
With love things never need to see an end,
only a new direction to travel.
Without Love we are not allowing ourselves
our humanity!

Eric Jackson 6/22/1990 ©

A Bit of Background
That Forms My Thinking

I was born in Brooklyn New York. My father, the wise man that he was, in the late 60's, had only one thought: "What's best for the kids?" So as soon as possible he moved my sister and me to the growing farm areas of Long Island New York to a town called Lake Ronkonkoma. I attended Sachem High School where I excelled in science and mathematics. I am an anatomy freak; I absorbed and kept hold of all of my science lessons far beyond any of the other schooling I encountered.

My scholastic goals were to become a chiropractor back in the 80's before any understanding of the art was truly accepted by modern medicine of the day.

23

Life ran its course and I became a product of the business environment that I grew up in.

Sitting here now at forty-five years old I am imagining myself utilizing whatever monies available to a convicted felon and going to school for something that causes me to major in the sciences. The thing is I know, *"it is never too late with structured goals."*

I reflect back to the elementary school only being an average student yet getting 100% plus all the extra credit answers in my science classes. It was so unusual for me that two of the smart kids in my class accused me of cheating on a 6th grade exam. My teacher Mr. Maier trusted that I had not cheated yet asked me if I would take the test again with new questions on the exact same topic. I gladly wished to prove my innocence. I took the test alone in a study area of Wenonah Elementary School. Once again I aced the test. Mr. Maier was so proud he came into the classroom and admonished my wrongful accusers by announcing to the entire class while specifically addressing Steven and Jeffery; "By the way, he not only got a score of 104 again but he spelled the same words wrong." Eugene Maier built confidence within me that day. I carry that support with me in my daily walk. He may have been aware of what he did for my confidence, but for me the understanding only came in my business ownership years, making sure that anyone that contributed to our success got public credit for their commitment.

When I hit my 8th grade year in Junior High School the same would apply. I received great grades in math and science. One story I recall in science class stands out to me. I spent the entire first week with my head down on the desk and my eyes closed. That Friday the third day of school the teacher gave us a quiz on the classroom work he had covered the two days previous. I aced it. The comment Monday when I put my head down while he handed back the quizzes was, "Jackson, I don't know what you think you are doing, but it is not going to go on in my classroom!" After class I approached him politely and explained "sometimes for me, hearing something with my eyes closed allows it to sink in my head much better." Letting him know the manner in which I was able to learn best made my argument successful. He never gave me any friction in his class for the remainder of the year. When I hit Sachem High School students moved into elective classes. I consistently choose the math and sciences to load my elective credits. The only English elective I opted for was Mr. Fabian's Publishing class; that was the year that my father and I were publishing **THE TRADER SPEAKS** a monthly baseball card and memorabilia magazine. I wanted to learn the technical aspects of the newspaper and magazine publishing trades, never realizing that some of those lessons would be guiding me today, as I sit here in my cell developing my cover layout.

One of the best classes I had was anatomy and physiology. Besides the teacher Fred Gilliam, being among the top 4 of my entire schooling, it included dissection which taught me much about the body's anatomy which stays with me in every way I think connected to medical situations to this day.

As most that went to schools that had science labs recognize, there always tended to be a best lab partner in class to choose. Well that was always me. I thrived on experiments. Biology, earth science, chemistry, physiology were all equally amazing to me, I loved them all. Most boys like chemistry because the teachers tend to allow the basic use of volatile chemicals which captures the attention of young male minds. I didn't have much excitement with the exploding Pepsi and breath mints. I guess now I understand why. Any fool can do that. For me it was all about understanding measure, time and temperature in chemistry. Also the wonders of the human body in biology, and how the study of animals led back to the understanding of how it related to us. Hair color of lab rats, types of cross breading of fruit flies and so on. Using the punnett squares, to determine what possible blood type my children may have or eye color, etc. This was long before the human genome project was even close to completion. These things intrigued me greatly. We had only learned the basics of the double helix and how they were beginning to understand the individual genes and what it was they may be responsible for in our individual genetic makeup.

Likely the reason I wanted, at that time, to go into chiropractic care was because of the basic interaction of the skeletal system with the body system as a whole was amazing to my mind. I surprise myself that I can write these things from the top of my mind in a jail cell thinking back over 30 years ago. Most people at 45, I would venture to guess would not remember 10th grade science class so clearly.

I also clearly remember back to the fourth grade, when the boys were sent to the gym and the girls went to the auditorium to watch a movie. I was the sole boy curious enough to go to the locker room to use the toilet and snuck off across the hall and sat quietly for the first time ever, (the quiet part, not the sneaking out part) in the back of the room and intently watched the movie on the female menstrual cycle, and how it worked. I doubt that I was more than eleven years old at the time. I am now 45 and I still remember this like it was yesterday. Further I am also 'that guy' who explains to my female friends how and why their cycles change and are sometimes late. I have always been the one who was taking my girlfriends to the gynecologist, often sitting and holding their hand through the appointment though sometimes I was over the doctor's shoulder watching and learning.

While my ex-wife was pregnant with our children was one of the greatest times of my life. Just being able to go through all the changes with her made me feel a part of something bigger than myself. The same took place with my best friend Tracie Vaughn during her pregnancy. I have always been very aware of the medical and scientific side of life. (Side note Palmers

Cocoa Butter really does prevent stretch marks and can be a very intimate encounter during pregnancy, don't neglect the boobs.)

Studying this subject of female ejaculation was just one more of those situations to me. I became so intrigued by the concept that I had to learn all that I could after figuring out I was pretty much able to make it happen to any woman that was comfortable with me and willing to openly communicate about sex.

At that point, for me most everything started out with a written goal. In this case it was as follows:

Lifetime Goal   8-15-2006

Somehow communicate to the masses what I have learned about female ejaculation and the need for open sexual communication within intimate relationships.

As the owner of a pizzeria at the time my 'mastermind group' was every adult male I ran into, which were plentiful. I would also discuss it with many of my female friends. I would ask the men a few brief questions, inquiring if they had ever been with a woman that had soaked the sheets during a sexual encounter to open the lines of communication and let it go from there. Many men would have no idea what I was talking about, but the few that were aware had a wide spectrum of comments.

> Mastermind Group – An assembly of 2 or more people discussing the development of a common idea.

We came up with many good ideas on how to achieve my goal and many unrealistic ones. About a year into discussing this subject on a near constant basis, one quality idea was move to Nevada and open a spa where married women would come from around the world to the spa for a week. They would spend the first few days in a classroom environment to study and learn how to accept the sensual experiences that occur in the bedroom without confusion or shame. Then we would have the husbands join on the last few days of

31

the stay for a few lessons followed by couple counseling with a sexual therapist to acquaint them with the information that their wives had discovered and expressed. Though my goals were to always allow for 'Female Ejaculation' as the outcome of quality communications, the true winning result would be the communication itself! I felt this idea was wonderful yet beyond my means at the time. It was always entertaining to talk about because all of the single men I spoke to said *"Let me be an instructor"*, I always laughed. That idea is still on my long term goal sheet for female ejaculation education.

Many people ask me "Eric, what makes you so cocky to say what makes an elevated sexual experience for a woman, you are not one?" I clearly am not a woman! But this is how I would address the question. I freely and openly communicate with women on the subject. Much of the study I performed from 2005 to 2007 was live survey. To address the female side of my study I found it most easy to use America Online chat rooms to conduct interviews. I would open up a *'User Created'* chat room that had a name that would revolve around *'female sexual survey'* or directly to the point *'female ejaculation'*.

I would ask women willing to express their experiences to instant message me so that we could talk privately and I could save the conversations for later study. Some conversations were just plain fake; others were clearly genuine and those women were in need of supportive communication. In some cases I was even able to make these women feel a little better. Many expressed shame and embarrassment with regard to their first and only ejaculating experiences, thinking that they had soaked the sheets with urine. To this day I still reply to any Yahoo Answers inquiry where women think that they urinated rather than it being a natural process of sexual stimulation and not urine. Others were very forthcoming and freely communicated their understanding of the process and explaining to me how it worked for them.

Negative experiences caused some women to never mentally get past that building up feeling again, thus retarding their sexual growth. A few even expressed that their boyfriends at the time verbally abused them, accusing them of ruining the bed and expelling them from the room and breaking up with them shortly thereafter.

A single incident of this type communication is disturbing, but it seemed that over the years of talking to women and men these results were not limited to the online chat.

Many men were not ashamed to say they dumped their lover due to this single factor of soaking the sheets with what they believed to be urine. This outcome, I felt to be sad, due to lack of understanding and mainstream awareness, the girls not knowing at all what just took place, but knowing it felt really good, many used the word amazing; while the men reacting negatively, causes their companion to feel ashamed and confused.

These females explained to me that they were very comfortable with their partners. Some were even the men that they had lost their virginity too. However the partners reacted to the abundant fluid as urine and were appalled by this little known natural bodily function; never considering it may have been as normal as male ejaculate. These stories made me sympathetic to the 'female cause'. Too many stories about young men yelling at or ending relationships with their girlfriends, due to the confusion surrounding this little discussed natural function.

Even though 'The G-Spot' book and connected medical studies were in the mass media since the early 80's, they were not completely understood. The more comfortable a girl was with her boyfriend the harder it was to take this level of rejection. The scorn which these females endured was often too much to ever allow the action to repeat itself. Many of these females, who were not sexually inhibited at that time, were then scorned for life. My goal was intensified to share the facts I learned about the subject. These encounters were even a larger motivation for me to find a way to communicate the truth that was so desperately needed.

Around October 2006 I began investigating further. I delved into the unreliable world of the Internet, where any fool can post their opinion regardless of how accurate it would be. Being a former web site developer I was aware of the downfall of this line of investigation, therefore my approach was very skeptical. My first web query (search term) was *female ejaculation*. The very first listing was a You Tube video of a young woman reading word for word the Wikipedia page on female ejaculation into a video camera.

I was not at that time aware of the existence of You Tube or Wikipedia; they were both new sites to me. Since exiting the web development business after 9/11 and going back to my roots of the pizza business I did not keep up on the development of these sites. You Tube started its development in February 2005 and

Wikipedia sometime in 2001. I was very let down when I went to these two sites; not in their development or function, just regarding the limited content for female ejaculation information. They offered identical information delivered in video and written form, yet fell short of what I had already know and much of the information was inaccurate considering the research which did exist in the market prior to that point.

As I learned more that Wikipedia, the public contribution encyclopedia, was based on only information submitted by those knowing how to make editing changes I understood the lack. Today in 2012 both Wikipedia and You Tube contain considerable information on female ejaculation and the accuracy is quite up to date. I have contributed to both these forums over the years.

At that time in '07 I was not aware of the medical work by Whipple and Perry or the book on the G-Spot and its relation to this topic. *To date as I sit in my cell writing this text I have not yet read or owned a copy of*

'The G-SPOT', my plan is to read it upon my release at some point prior to publishing this text. My motivating experience was only the one time it happened to me when I was 20, and the book I read in 1999 by Tom Leonardi explaining his experience. The years in my marriage and with Michele never yielded an ejaculating orgasm. But by 2007 and through 2009 I was able to cause all of my intimate partners to learn to ejaculate while researching the subject. Five out of five personally and I indirectly succeeded in instructing 4 others. I knew this was real as well as learnable and teachable.

I always had a passionate faith that I would be delivered the tools needed to deliver the message within my lifetime goal. For me in life things continually aligned when I would follow my goals with passion. At this point on 2/19/2012 I even consider the last 7 years of turmoil connected to the lies of Michele and loss of my freedoms, her coercive father as well as the negativity that he attracted in his personal goal, as a *gift to me.*

Had I remained in the Pizza Business in the South Jersey area there would be no way to continue to earn a quality living due to the foolish pricing within the local pizza market. Selling pizza as a loss leader to drive customers into the business, my competition hoped to profit on sandwiches and fried sides which had inflated pricing. I would still be fighting a losing battle. In the *big picture of life* we are led down many paths which we are dissatisfied taking, but most times a positive mental perspective will provide you alternatives if you have a keen eye. "Thanks go to Howard and Michele for destroying my former path, sending me on this journey."

Upon closing the pizza place in March of 2007 I moved into the security camera business which was profitable, while working to complete my DVD. The life experience which brought me to putting these words to paper... so many small adjustments in my world made over the past 30 years I truly could not account for without the oversight of a higher universal power.

From the time I was 17 and convinced my father to endeavor into the publishing business I now feel I may just have been a puppet in the play of my own life. Not to say I didn't have control to go in any direction, but for the most part I behaved in a good service manner treating others with love and expecting little in return beyond their business or company. I was delivered great riches at various times in my life, in my pizza and computer career from 1987 to 2007 in the form of dollars but mostly my rewards were the relationships I developed over those years. Also, the positive direction I personally was able to influence so many young minds. Even today here in jail I run into guards as well as inmates that were former customers and receive compliments on how good a business Echo Pizza was and memories they carry from the positive experiences.

Perhaps this endeavor into being a mentor began for me in high school when chosen to be a *Student Teacher* from my 10th grade math class. There was a program where the teachers would select one student to teach all their classes for the day. I was chosen because I exhibited something to Joseph Sabatino of Sachem High School on Long Island, New York. He saw something in me that others had not, something that the other students had not demonstrated. I had passion. I had the passion to learn as well as the passion to teach. Joe then and there showed me the value of being a teacher in life.

Mr. Sabatino was our geometry teacher and the students in my class had heard that he had other money beyond his job and wondered why he taught. Now I understand if that was a true statement of his financial independence, he did it for the love of teaching and the passion he had for developing young minds. Those passions were god given in my opinion, and a greater reward than money.

My skill in the pizza business was the ability to break the processes down into their simplest terms, allowing others to repeat the process, lessons taught in that 10th grade class room. This is also what allows my instructional DVD program to take a step beyond the other similar video programs out there. My education in the pizza business was also a building block on which the DVD was produced, breaking orgasmic expulsion into its simplest terms, so that anyone can understand.

Questions and My Answers

Over the years I have answered many questions about Female Ejaculation, this chapter will share a handful of these, to summarize what I have to say on the subject. So if you have chosen to read this book because of the title and do not opt to purchase the DVD Instructional program I believe that the questions along with my answers may guide your mind to have a better understanding of process associated with female ejaculation. *However, I feel strongly there is no better tool than the instructional video viewed together as a couple.* My answers will also allow you the reader to quickly vet my position on the subject.

Female Ejaculation.....?

I am able to ejaculate and have been able to for some time now but I have found I can only release it when I'm in the shower or over a toilet.. This is frustrating since me and my boyfriend and I would like for it to happen in the bedroom but something stops me no matter what I have tried.

Has anyone got any advice or anything for this situation?

Additional Information from Asker

I mean I can ejaculate with him in the shower.. just not out of the shower as if my mind doesn't let me because I'm not used to weeing somewhere like my room so I can't squirt in there either. Just need to get that out of my head really.

Answer

This is just a suggestion from my experience. I teach female ejaculation for a living. I called my DVD product THE BIG SOAK. I say this for a serious reason. I believe your head will not allow you to soak the bed, couch or other. First give it a try on the kitchen floor with a towel. Then it may help you with your mental block. Next, consider if you have not already been doing....put 2 big fluffy towels under your butt before you start fooling around. Have him work your g-area until you can't help but let go as you know how in the toilet. You might find it to be the best ejaculating orgasm you have ever had, because of the conflict of your brain if you actually let it out in the bed on the towels, it may unblock your hesitation...

Just a thought, good luck...

During sex, weird liquid coming out of me?

Okay so I was having sex with my boyfriend and we were doing it doggy style and for some freaky weird reason this watery liquid came out of my vagina... It wasn't the normal lubricating liquid that happens before and during sex. I didn't pee myself, we both saw it and felt it come out of there. I wasn't anywhere near orgasm so I couldn't have "squirted". It has never happened before. I have NO idea what happened. Does anyone??? It's just such a weird thing.

Thank you.

Answer

Female ejaculate! (You did squirt) like pre-come in a guy, I have seen it just start flowing from women, especially in that position because of the pressure on you G-area.

Do all women squirt / ejaculate?

Well, I'm trying to be as serious as possible.. And trying to not be rude.. I don't know if "Ejaculation" would be the correct term.. but.. Back to business, do all females.. "Squirt"?

Answer

Very Sadly - Most Can; but many psych themselves out, their mind preventing it from taking place because nobody ever told them it was totally normal.

Yet, Most if not all women CAN, in my opinion. It is a very tricky question.

I believe female ejaculation is a completely normal function of the human body and I convey this in my work.

As a Sex Educator, specializing in Female Ejaculation, I have found that it is all about the trust and comfort within the relationship.

If you are in a situation with a woman who has trust in you, and who is comfortable enough with her own sexuality then she will respond very well to techniques of G-area stimulation.

If however there is any lack of trust and or any sexual inhibitions there is very little chance of her experiencing the quality orgasm that accompanies ejaculation.

Younger girls 17-20 as well as older 35+ women are more easily instructed in this area.

The reasons seem to be that the younger ones that have not ejaculated, if told it is OK will go with the flow... older women seem to search it out based on not being able to achieve consistent fulfilling orgasms by themselves or with a partner.

The best thing is to get some expert book or video like mine or similar, so the lines of communication within the relationship are opened and the subject matter is more comfortable.

Good luck.

Are there side effects of too much female ejaculation?

I am a female 24 year old female, and I wanna know the side effects of too much female ejaculation?

Answer

YES...

Better health both mental and physical, a well flushed out lymphatic system, increased Endorphins, considerably less stress, and reduction of chronic pain via the release of Oxytocin.

These side effects are all positive!

The only negative side effect is very wet towels or sheets and having to do a bit more laundry.

Good Luck

Can you squirt before you orgasm?

I have really been wanting to squirt. I've heard it is amazing! So I've done some research and my bf and I tried it. Well there is definitely a lot of clear liquid that comes out. Like a cup full. But it doesn't shoot out or squirt out in a stream it kinda just rushes out. And it happens before not during my orgasm. I want one of those full body orgasms! And I know my bf would love it if it shot out and didn't just fill his hand up I know I'm not peeing. There is no color or smell, so why does it come out that way and too soon? Sorry if it's TMI but I need to know!

Answer

Not TMI good question. What you are saying is basically that you are continuing to ejaculate but prior to orgasm. Understand this (the BF) just like on a penis you must hold the pressure in to create the buildup. He needs to learn to feel when the gushing is about to begin and apply more pressure to prevent its flow but not stop moving around inside to keep the pleasure. He needs to picture himself masturbating and how he holds back so there is a more powerful orgasm by not allowing the ejaculation to just drip out but pressure building by squeezing and pushing. I think once he has this in his *head and you understand what the goal is you will have no problem shooting far past the bed from where you are already just from a little reading... great communication on both your part. GO FOR IT!*

How can you tell if you have a female ejaculation?

I've had orgasms but only through my clit. But I've never had an orgasm through the g-area or sex...so I don't know if I have the female ejaculation and I would like to know how can you tell? Does it happen EVERY TIME you have an orgasm? Do u have it or have u had a girlfriend like that?

Answer

Well starting out it should be easy to see if there was female ejaculation. The wet spot will be larger than a small plate. If the wet spot is just a sliver then it is likely that you have not.

You need to relate your body to what you can see on a man. We men are built from women at conception yet our parts are on the outside and easy to see and play with.

The clitoris is like the head of the male penis. It can be overstimulated! To the degree that you just can't handle how good it feels and you reach the peek, and stop at the climax.

The shaft of the penis, the underside to be specific, is equivalent to what's known as the g-area. It's an area just inside the vagina and runs in the general direction of the belly button. The glands and nerve endings that surround the urethra in a woman are the same as what is found in men. These glands fill with fluid and become engorged in women the same way as in men. With the right stimulation ejaculation is forthcoming just like in men. With some study and understanding most all women can ejaculate.

It can happen every time if you practice and understand what the feelings leading up to the orgasmic expulsion that is known as female ejaculation.

Hope this answers some of your question.

Would it bother another woman if her partner has a female ejaculation?

Because, you see, I don't know if I can have one, but in case I do, is that embarrassing? I mean, if she's giving me oral sex and suddenly--yeah.

My girlfriend--future wife--knows I don't believe in sex before marriage, and I don't masturbate either, so I don't know if I'm capable of a female ejaculation. Thanks in advance for any help.

Answer

It may bother her if she never saw or heard of it. She will be cool with it if you first discuss and COMMUNICATE with your future life partner. As an expert in teaching female ejaculation I can tell you for sure communication on the subject as well as a little education is all that is needed to be prepared if it does happen.

It would likely be my goal in any straight relationship from the time I learned it could happen to communicate with my partner. You seem somewhat informed, so the two of you should learn how to have this fantastic orgasm. It is mostly a learned thing yet it seems only the rare women allow it to happen naturally, without some study or research on the subject.

Female Ejaculation Question?

During sex it feels like I really need to pee. I've gone to the toilet just before sex but it still feels like I'm going to wet myself. I looked into it and apparently this feeling is g-spot stimulation and if continued you squirt. That would be fine. I usually stop when I feel the needing to pee sensation though or put myself in a position where I can't really feel the sex all that much because I'm too scared that I might pee on him. My boyfriend keeps trying to encourage me to just let go and squirt but I'm too scared that I'd actually pee. That would be horrific for me. How can I make sure I don't pee?

Answer

Though in advance of the actual occurrence it is difficult to put your mind to rest, you may feel better giving in and trusting him. He is looking forward to discovering this natural body response to sexual stimulation. You have already disclaimed that you empty your bladder prior to sex, so relax and let it go. Put a big fluffy towel down first under your butt, and do the sniff test afterwards. I am very confident that it is not urine and you will not pee on him, it sounds like he is pretty sure as well.

What are some positions or techniques to make it happen?

How come I can never get an orgasm?!
It takes so much work that... My bf gets soft ahah and I tell him that he's getting closer...so basically I'm just making a lot of fake noises but I think it makes him feel manly ha-ha

I really want to get one with him, I've only had sex 4 times so far this month and so far in my life ha-ha what are some positions or techniques to make it happen??

Answer

It is never healthy to outright deceive your partner, especially in the bedroom. This could cause harm to the relationship that may not be able to be recovered from.

I first suggest that you consider getting a book on positions, maybe More Joy of Sex by Alex Comfort, MD, The Man's Gourmet Sex Book by the Burke's, Hot Sex by Tracey Cox, or The Karma-Sutra book and investigate with him some of the positions. Maybe get it for a present or ask him to get it for you as a present. With a little bit of fun in the request, I would think he would be happy not hurt. It is very confusing because there is such conflicting information on the female orgasm. [Many will say it is in the mind of the woman not the body? To me this is not the answer.] I have heard women tell me after having an ejaculating orgasm that this is the "real deal" Now these same women have believed that they had been orgasmic in the past, yet after an ejaculating orgasm they feel that now they know what an orgasm is. So you are not alone in this feeling of 'un-sureness'... Many women are unsure and fake their way through sexual relations.

I want to 'squirt' for my boyfriend!?

My man, like all men, is super into the female ejaculation aka squirting thing and I have read into this a lot lately but was just wondering if there are any female readers who can do this? And maybe can give me pointers on how I can learn? My friend can do it but she says that it just comes naturally and that u can't learn it. But articles I've read online say that u can u just have to know the right spot? Please help me?

Answer

It is true, as of the past 5 years many more men are looking for the squirt... THAT IS A GOOD THING!! I love that you are asking -- which is the first hurdle most females need to overcome, TALK ABOUT IT. Love that you asked your girlfriend and she had an

answer, but I am confident that it can be learned! Love
that you are reading up on the topic... Keep up the
study and you will find all that you need. It is a learned
response to sexual stimulation, I think your friend is
wrong and it can be learned. You will first get to the
point that you feel like you are about to urinate. I
assure you, YOU WON'T. If you can get past that
feeling and just relax and let go you are on your way.

Good Luck and Good Sex

Having to stop before orgasm?

I'm new to sex and every time my partner pleasures
me, by rubbing my clit etc. I have to get him to stop
after a certain period of time because it feels like I can't
take it anymore. Is this normal? How can I make this
needing to stop feeling go away?

Kind of a weird question ha-ha but thanks

Answer

Often women masturbate by rubbing their clitoris
and therefore men think this is also the manner that

they enjoy sexual stimulation best! Men often get carried away with rubbing this area to the point it is overstimulated and even raw. I often equate to men if you had a girl licking or rubbing just the head of your penis would you not eventually have to make them stop? Not because it doesn't feel good but it gets too intense and overstimulated? Most men answer yes. There is an area on the upper inside wall of the vagina that is known as the g-spot (area) and stimulation of this area is a better area to concentrate on. The agreed opinion is that stimulation of this area causes increased sexual stimulation. This area is also mostly responsible for female ejaculation if stimulated correctly and in a relationship where there is comfortable communications between partners.

If you would like to learn more do some study and have him help you so he understands as well.

Good luck and Good orgasms!!

Did I have a mind orgasm?

The other day me and my bf were kissing, and I had a button down shirt on, and he put his mouth to my breasts.... And I hear you can get an orgasm virtually anywhere... And as he was doing work I guess I'll call it, I felt this incredible rush in my head.. It worked just like an orgasm.. It was building up in my mind until I got this incredible feeling in my head, then I got dizzy after that, cuz I usually get that after I have a regular orgasm... Is this normal? Or even possible?

Answer

Totally normal, there are varying levels to orgasmic feelings! Possible too, a percentage of women in lab situations with electrodes on their heads and vagina have been tested and are able to have full vaginally contracting orgasms by simply looking at sexual images and thinking sexual thoughts. Men are not so talented. Though I personally have been in some situations where I am down on my girl and without any physical contact to my penis, I have had a full ejaculating orgasm. So I would say our minds have much more to do with our sexual feelings and orgasm than science has yet discovered. Women's minds are much more in tune with their bodies so YES you likely did climax from the boob play.

How can I tell my boyfriend he has never made me orgasm?

I am really in love with my boyfriend and I really enjoy sex with him and it does feel nice but he has never made me orgasm. Should I tell him and if so how? I don't want to hurt his feelings but I want to be able to share that kind of intimacy better with him.

Thanks

Answer

Telling him may bruise his male ego... instead consider buying a book or video, on the g-spot and female ejaculation. He will likely get interested and learn some new techniques on his own....coach him on what feels good and get him to listen when you teach by being firm and understanding... play it a little dumb, not to insult or dishearten him..."I don't know, when you do that it feels so good", or "I don't know, when you do that I don't really feel anything..." just a thought...

Is it normal to have a watery discharge when you have an orgasm?

Just like it asks? When I come I have like water come out and I didn't know it was normal or not?

Answer

It is called female ejaculation... congrats. Put a towel down from now on.... totally natural response to vaginal orgasm.

The inside of my vagina is swollen?

Yesterday and the day before, I was with my bf. We messed around a lot and had a lot of sex. We hadn't been able to see each other for a while due to work, so we got out all the sexual frustration while we could. Yesterday I noticed a slight tenderness, but that happens a lot after we have sex. We tend to be a little rough. The tenderness always goes away, though, the next day. I woke up this morning and the inside of my vagina is VERY swollen. I felt inside to see if there was any discharge, and there was none. But I did notice that it would hurt to put two fingers in. No smell or anything. It's just swollen. It doesn't itch. There's tenderness outside of the vagina, but that's not really bad at all, just slightly uncomfortable if I mess with it. Yesterday after I came back home, I also noticed a mucus type substance and looked it up, but from what I found that should just be a sign of me ovulating. There's also cramping that comes and goes, it's somewhere between a sharp pain and a dull ache. From what I know I'm not allergic to latex. I mean, I use latex gloves all the time, and it's not the first time we had sex with a latex condom, and I've never had a reaction before.

I'm working, and I work 24/5, so I can't exactly go to the doctor right now. So I'd like to get some idea of what's wrong. Any ideas? Any ways I can at least help the swelling?

Answer

It is likely your Urethral Sponge, aka the Female Prostate. This area is on the front wall inside of your vagina. It surrounds the urethra. It swells with fluid from sexual friction on the g-area...

If you are a non-ejaculating woman you can relax it is just swollen from pleasure.... It will slowly subside...

You may want to read a bit on female ejaculation because it sounds to me like you can...

The pain was likely you getting swollen inside and him pulling out then trying to get back in.

Which wall in the vagina is the most touch sensitive?

Is there a specific wall in the vagina that feels better when the penis rubs on it? Like the top, bottom, left or right wall inside the vagina? Or is it just all of it?

Answer

Upper wall between the vaginal opening and the belly button is the most receptive to touch/contact.

Orgasm and losing bodily function?

My girlfriend when she has multiple orgasms she loses bodily function at the back door. If you know what I mean. Is that normal, if not how do you control it?

Answer

It is not common because most women are not comfortable enough with their relationship to continue through the pleasurable feelings of orgasm. Most women will stop the stimulation and change positions to prevent the loss of bowel muscle control. The high tension between contractions and bliss cause the inability of control.. If you are not freaked out by this than put down a towel first.. As they often say sex is HOT STEAMY AND MESSY..... there is no such thing as normal in the bedroom and there is further no such thing as normal when it comes to women in bed.... every good thing is just that a good thing... but it is up to each individual to determine what is good or not.... you seem to be ok with it…

How Can I Make Myself Squirt?

I have been trying to do it for ages now, by myself and with my boyfriend, I have had the sensation many a times with my boyfriend, but I always either hold it in, or I ignore it, as I get scared, as I am worried about peeing all over him!! Help, how can I do it myself? And be SUCCESSFUL?? I've done all the G-Spot stimulating etc., can anyone on here squirt, if so, how do you do it? Please HELP ME!!!

Answer

From what you are describing you are close. So if you are just worried consider trying it in the shower first. This location change may allow you to not let your head get in the way. Much of sex is in the mind and we humans often cannot get past our own brains. It occurs with men in the premature ejaculation department and sometimes Erectile Dysfunction is a mental block. In this case I feel your head is preventing your body from relaxing and letting go. If you can try it in the shower you may be able to become more comfortable with the feelings inside your body without your head getting in the way.

Um....How Do Guys Feel About... Squirting?

So I recently was messing around with my boyfriend and suddenly had the urge to pee really badly, so I stopped what we were doing and tried to go, but I didn't actually have to.

I looked it up and found out that means I'm probably a squirter, and later that night I confirmed it myself hah.

How do guys feel about female ejaculation?

How do I bring it up to him or "warn" him next time?

Answer

Some men are informed enough to know it is a real orgasm and not urine. They love female ejaculation, aka squirting, gushing, orgasmic expulsion, and many others.

The public in general are sadly misinformed about this totally natural response to quality love making. Communication is the missing link.

Your best bet is to just talk to him and ask if he has ever had a squirter, before? Let him know that he brought you to the point you were about to come in that way, but were unsure what he would think... perhaps show him what you can achieve yourself...

Can a woman orgasm if I lick or finger her vagina long enough?

No penetration needed? Can she orgasm again if we have sex after? Will she squirt?

Answer

For sure yes, most women can come from oral sex and minor vaginal stimulation....

As far as female ejaculation (squirting) you need to understand the positioning and procedure of g-area stimulation.

You will also need to communicate with her on the squirting matter because most girls will not squirt unless they have discussed it first and understand what is happening. Open communication is the key to female ejaculation.. Many women are multi-orgasmic and need little recovery time in comparison to men.

Female ejaculation! I love it my boyfriend hates it?

My boyfriend and I don't normally disagree like this. But he hates the idea of Female Ejaculation he won't talk to me about it or listen to me he just shuts off. Problem is its one of my favorite things I love it. I just feel ashamed of myself now I can't have sex with him because I'm scared it will happen and he will get mad at me.

P.S. I don't need answers telling me women can't ejaculate etc. I know women can. Try it before you close your mind and think you know everything about it.

Answer
Sorry to hear that you are having a problem like this. However I find in my study of hundreds of men there is about 30 percent of those surveyed would rather avoid it if possible. I am not sure why. I searched it out with every girlfriend since I knew it was a reality at age 20. I am now 44 and teach the techniques for a living.

So as expert in this subject matter I can give you some sound advice. Invest $20 into my or some other Sex Education DVD on female ejaculation. It would I think be worth its weight in gold for the opening of a dialog after watching the factual and real information on the subject in a 30 min video format that guys usually take as porn of some sort because they get to see vagina....

But if 30 minutes of hearing some other people talk about what you already KNOW to BE FACT doesn't open his mind not sure how to, at least it will plant a seed. Women should and can ejaculate at the height of orgasm in the same way a man can, with a physical expelling of fluids.

Also put down a towel while having any sexual relations just in case it does happen you won't kill his sheets and he will be able to use the towel at hand....

Good luck... some of my articles go into the reasons men don't get it, sometimes...

Asker's Comment:

*Thanks   :)   I'll   give   it   a   shot.
It's a shame more people are not open to the
experience. I'm glad you're spreading the word in
a positive way, there is too much negative stuff
associated with female ejaculation that just isn't
true.*

I was trying to get an orgasm that squirts, but how do I know that the fluid isn't just pee?

*I have tried this, a couple of times, and I use a
vibrating dildo. When I masturbate I get this feeling
that I have to pee. Suddenly the feeling goes away and I
squirt. I have read that it is supposed to be that way, but
I'm still not sure if the fluid is pee or the real deal.. How
do I know??? I also tried to sniff it, but I can't tell if it
is pee or not.*

Answer

As a standard it is rarely urine. There are times that it can have a slight salty smell depending on how hydrated your body is at the time of ejaculation. It is like you sweat. It is fluid from the glandular systems of your body not from your bladder. The swelling you feel inside is the buildup of prostate fluid inside your para-urethral sponge (updated aka Female Prostate). This build up expels as a gush or squirt from the urethra, where you pee from but it originates below your bladder in the Glands that surround your urethra. This is the reason many think it is urine is because it is expelled in the same way.

While men never concern themselves with the worry did they pee or ejaculate because the fluid is thick and goopy because it protects the sperm in the high acid of the vaginal canal. Female Ejaculate has the consistence of water, yet it has been tested in labs and contains PSA a chemical that is only found in male ejaculate from what was previously known. The discovery of PSA *(prostate specific antigen) allowed scientists to re-name the Glands surrounding the woman's urethra the Female Prostate because it was the only explanation as to the presence of these PSA chemicals.   Yet in laboratory data collection they have only produced for study 3-4 cc of milky white fluids, I think that is because they are in a lab...*

"Those Who Judge Don't Matter

Those Who Matter Don't Judge!"
Shared by Miss Jackie
Originally by Anonymous

Goal Setting

Since the very first success, planning was required! Without a plan which we will now learn to transform to the goal, there is little chance for a successful outcome. If one chooses to use the bathroom, you must first plan in your mind which way your body needs to carry you. As well when you finish you would be foolish to hope there was toilet paper if you need to use some to wipe yourself. These are two examples in simplest terms. We rarely realize how much we plan in our everyday tasks.

Setting goals, however, is a bit different. There is a proven system for success, as well as failure. The expression 'fail to plan, and plan on failing', in my opinion, fell a little short of what is necessary for assured success. Success is much more assured with the use of goals incorporated into your plan. Plans and goals both start out the same. An idea hits the brain and there is a need somewhere deep inside to follow the mind's eye.

Some of us were taught at a very young age to follow our own mental vision, others however were taught just the opposite: "Be seen and not heard." This means starting around 4 years old until sometimes ages 18 to 23 years old and out of college, a direction was dictated. The latter group was always told what to say, how to think and perform, never allowing their own mind's eye position to be realized. Ideas came and went with no real belief that they could ever really be achieved.

But those of us, who were supported in our mind's eye visions, were very lucky our parental guidance was flexible and supportive. That simple act of allowing the youthful brain to become the independent leader of our lives is perhaps the greatest gift of all.

With that understood, let's see if you are the first group or the second. Think back to your childhood.

Were you encouraged?

Or, did someone constantly tell you?: "That's a pipe dream"; "Never going to happen"; "Can't do that, it's too risky"; "Get your head out of the clouds". If you are reading this you are now self-motivated without a doubt, yet think how many years of catching up you need. You need to retrain your brain to eliminate the previous programing. You need an updated operating system, believing in yourself and the possibilities that are out there for all of us. Reprogram your neurons to achieve the impossible heights other in this world do, if others do it, maybe it really is not impossible!

Believing naysayers, you - yourself let your mind's idea go right past you. You, actually choosing to listen to these negative expressions, plant the seeds of doubt suffocating your own dreams. Believing these words prevented you from following your own dreams and what was inside your head, often breaking your spirit of individual thought. If however, you were to *'write down the idea and treat it as a possibility'* the moment you thought of it, those terms of negative influence may have left your brain. Your written goal could have, even if completely crazy or far-fetched, allowed you to invent, create or start your own: whatever...

Even if your idea seems impossible, as long as there is reasonable thinking and logic behind its origin *write it down.* Your brain will start acting on the written words and notice things that may make your impossible goal attainable at some point; you must be receptive to various means that present themselves.

Writing goals and ignoring the negative input perhaps would have allowed you to control your own destiny, rather than having your life left in the hands of others to control.

To solidify a goal, one must follow further steps. These go beyond just writing them down. It starts with the written word, which will begin to sensitize multiple centers in your brain. First the visual centers; which is far different than just thinking up a plan. The next step your need to follow is to post the written goal in a place where you can see it *prominently*. So now you have step 1, think up your plan; step 2, transfer your plan to writing; step 3, place your new goal sheet in a place where you can see it multiple times daily.

Fourth, the next center of your brain that will be attacked is the auditory centers. You need to read the goal out loud at least once daily, the more the better. This transforms the way in which your brain understands and comprehends the written word. This is perhaps the most important of the steps in accomplishing your goal. I cannot emphasize enough the importance of step 4. The last of the steps, step 5 completes the process of sending you on your way to achieving your goals, no matter how far-fetched they may be. You must blend these first four steps with *passionate belief.* The passion to achieve your goal will cause you to become a magnet, actually attracting the tools, people and funding needed to achieve that goal.

I can only speculate how the fifth step affects your brain, but for sure without a doubt it has clearly made a difference in my accomplishment of the many wild ideas I have ever had over the past thirty years of successful ventures.

Passion is also how my advisories succeeded in the negative goals that lead my life down a very different path than I had in mind. The following pages will relate how the use and application of positive goals directed my life to this point. Also, it will demonstrate that a goal does not need to be positive to be achieved when mixed with enough passion.

My first marked *goal directed* success was at age 18. I was written up in USA Today's Sports section on June

21st 1985. The five steps mapped out above made this possible as well as what got me there. I had not yet formally learned the five steps.

Once I realized that my idea was going to happen I contacted USA Today. I told the switchboard what I was doing they connected me to a writer named Steve Woodward. He told me he was interested yet I needed to call back the day before the event and he would get me into the Friday paper. I simply wrote down his name and extension number with the date 6-20-1985 big on the top. I taped it to my mirror so I would not neglect this important step in marketing and public relations.

My idea, to re-unite the 1969 Miracle Mets, which at the time was next to impossible, for many reasons. Yet just like the Mets themselves back in 1969 I passionately believed it could happen. I had been in the baseball card & collectables industry as the son of a well-known dealer and the kid that had been around forever. I started in the business with my father in 1978 at age 11 and continued throughout. I had been the kid that show promoters used to collect the autograph tickets making sure that the customer was not slipping anything by for free. I always did well and kept the lines moving smoothly. My reward was to get anything I wanted autographed for free, just one item. *In hindsight sitting with players like Joe DiMaggio, Pete Rose, Mickey Mantle, Duke Snyder I should have been a bad boy and gotten as many things signed as possible... but even then reputation was the thing my father instilled into my head more than other discipline.* Back to the point, I had a very good understanding at a very young age how the flow of people moved and where the lag points in the long lines were. I felt that I was going to be able to pull off having over a dozen players in the same building signing all at once. I was the one person in my mind that could pull it off. Not because at 18 years old I set a goal or knew anything about them. Not because I was better than any of the other professional show promoters of the time. Just simply because I believed with passion that I would be able to lead a staff to control a dozen people in the way I ran my autograph sessions when working for someone else. So even though I did not ever write down the idea of running a baseball card show I did drop all other things and work on only this event from the moment I came up with the idea, so I had the passion covered.

I was crystal clear on what I wanted. A show with 15 -20 of the best dealers, and as many of the 69 Mets that my dad's budget could afford get to Manhattan for the weekend. When I brought the idea to some colleagues that I had worked for in the past collecting autograph tickets at their show, they basically told me, it was a pipe dream, impossible to control that many players signing in a single session. Even at that age just one year out of high school I was very cocky.

My first connection was my father, I was previously in business with him publishing a baseball card monthly magazine called *THE TRADER SPEAKS* which I convinced him to purchase from a local friend of his, who was at the end of his publishing days. If at that time I had no true awareness of goals and how they worked, if I did the paper may still be in print.

Left to right: Sonny Jackson (dad), Al Weis, Cal Koonse, Jim McAndrew, Gary Gentry, Donn Clendendon, Eric Jackson, Cleon Jones, Tommie Agee, Ed Kranepool, Wayne Garrett, Don Cardwell. Photo by Eric Jackson in the Heisman Room of the Down Town Athletic Club.

The baseball card magazine allowed me to meet and interact with Ed Kranepool of the Mets. My dad contacted him and proposed my idea. The event was a complete success. Using a cafeteria style autograph room where a fan could purchase a single autograph or the entire 16 player package and wait in a single line while each player signed for them. This instance may be a glimpse into the level of passion and single mindedness needed to realize your goals.

I learned about goals later, and why I made it to USA Today. I purchased a no money down real estate course by Ed Beckley later that year at 19 years old. I was not aware of the value of goals at that point. This simple book and tape course demonstrated how the writing and reading could transform a dream into a goal. Not that this was original information that Beckley was delivering, but it was for me!

Learning something for the first time is somewhat like putting on much needed eye glasses. All of a sudden things become in focus in a different way. It is something like when I was playing with my father's glasses at a harbor side seafood restaurant in Port Jefferson, NY and all of a sudden I said "Wow, I need glasses, I didn't know that the boats out there had masts!" My mom and dad were surprised, I was amazed and in awe of the new sight in front of my eyes. At 19 I all of a sudden was able to see clearly for the first time in years. Now I should have noticed, when I couldn't read the road signs and passed by my exit often, that my vision was going downhill, but I missed that too I probably blamed it on the marijuana.

I was very good at getting what I put my mind to, even as a kid inside the mostly adult industry of buying and selling baseball cards and memorabilia. I also am sure if I had understood *goal setting* at 11 or 12 years old I could have made thousands of dollars each weekend instead of the couple of hundred that I actually did clear. I would have had a target not just in my head but in writing. Each time I made the target it would or could have expanded, perhaps even to surpass my dad and his collection.

After reading and listening to the books and tapes that Ed Beckley had assembled I quickly could see a whole new picture, when it had to do with making business and life plans. I began keeping journals and began the habit of writing goals on paper and posting them in a place I could see them.

Sometimes, understanding a <u>single thought</u> in life, <u>differently</u> than we have, can change everything. This is worth repeating. Sometimes, understanding a single thought in life, differently than we have, can change everything. The brain interprets reality only within the scope of the individuals' current comprehension. As when our eyes trick us due to only seeing a partial or obstructed image, we believe the image to be something other than what it truly is, until the obstruction is removed and the picture is complete. We use adaptive thought to complete the picture from what we have stored in our brain. Once we realize our own interpretations misled us we laugh at our original thinking.

For me this single new skill of using my pen and the guidelines of goal setting, created a pizza business second to none in Voorhees New Jersey. For two decades Echo Pizza was king because of our weekly meetings and the goal setting sessions.

Later around 21 I read THINK AND GROW RICH by Napoleon Hill which was published in the late 1930's and I realized where Ed Beckley got most of his information about goals, it worked even if second hand. Hill's publication was and is the greatest book ever written on goal achievement and putting what he called *"burning desire"* behind your goal.

My second marked success on my resume came while in a rut working at Domino's Pizza. I now see that out of adversity comes advancement. While traveling from New York to Westchester, PA to consider a management position for a store in that area with a supervisor friend Alan Goldner, my companions and I took a side trip to Atlantic City. We stopped to eat on the way back at the Silver Coin Diner in Hammonton New Jersey. They also worked for Domino's, I began the discussion of whether staying with Domino's was a good idea. They convinced me to go forward with the move and the better position at Domino's. However I did ask the waitress for a pen. I flipped over the placemat on the table and started jotting down my goals as instructed in Beckley's course. The first was to buy a twin house for no money down, where I could live and rent the other half to cover a majority of the bills. The second was to open a pizza place somewhere in the North East United States that had no more than 5 competitors and a High School in the delivery area. 36 days later I owned a pizza place in Voorhees, New Jersey. The goals were written on the 16th of April 1987, I closed escrow on my first commercial rental property at 20 years old on May 22, 1987. And, it was a *'no money down'* deal which my father even doubted could happen; although a huge supporter of the Mets re-union 2 years before, he said "Who's going to give you their business for no cash down?" That part of the goal on the twin house was written just one line above the goal for the pizza place. I owe Ansar and Anjum Ahmed great thanks for believing that I could succeed where they had not. Over the seven years following, from 1987 to 1994 the entire business model was based on goal oriented foundations. The entire staff was goal driven and credited for the overall success of the business.

This started with the giant graph plotting the 52 weeks of the year covering almost 6' wide x 3' high of the office wall inside the pizza shop. In plain sight, written where every employee could see it daily and measure the improvement of the business.

My new personal goals for that time were the manner in which my staff and I would handle customer service. If a customer didn't like the pizza for any reason I would bring them their money back, personally. *(I reflected upon the lesson my dad gave me on reputation and how important it is for long term business, I offer that same money back guarantee with this book as well as my DVD.)* The manner in which book keeping would be maintained, how each individual on my staff would be personally responsible to market and bring sales into the business and support their own payroll while building a consumer base.

Each of the above items was expanded and on a numbered goal list next to the sales graph. The graph being the strongest motivation of all solely for its overpowering size, it was written and there was no confusion recognizing our advancements. Sales at that business rose from $1,500 a week when I took over to over $15,000 per week, almost $70,000 per month at the time I sold just seven years later for $325,000.00, thanks to the setting and follow through with goals. Due to mismanagement and failure to follow the system of success laid out, by the new owner, the business was in receivership in less than 2 years.

My only mistake in that business was not setting the lofty goal of purchasing the shopping center where the business was located! I recommend anyone venturing into small business set the long term goal of somehow buying a property themselves, collecting rent from themselves instead of paying someone else's mortgage. Had I added purchasing the property to my list of lofty goals I would likely still own that property to this day, even if I had left the restaurant business. So listen up and take some good advice, if you own a business but you rent the property, you are working for your landlord.... BUY THE LAND and THE BRICKS!

All of a sudden in 1990 we were profitable at the business. It was so unbelievable to my manager Michael Howe and me; we actually went together to the bank to check that there was not an accounting error on their part because there was an exorbitant amount of money in our account. One of my accounting goals was never balance the check book; the negative numbers were too depressing in the early years. *"One knows they have arrived at success when they no longer have to hope the check clears!"*

This to me was financial stability! LOL. I now understand there is no such thing as financial stability, except forms of residual income. Things like this book, or my DVD, which my great grandchildren may still be selling without any investment what-so-ever, beyond the manufacture cost.

Back to the point, with my newly perceived financial stability illusion, I set out to find the love of my life, marry, and have lots of kids! I started developing ideas of what this woman would look like, act like, and think like; what her sexual behaviors would be like; what her family values would be like.

That was the goal and shortly thereafter, I met the girl of those dreams. Wow! I was head over heels in love, again following my goals that had been written. There were no downfalls in my mind. Little did I know, marital relationships are not tangible items that can be awarded to the persistent, those that have not yet learned the skills needed for quality communication. Successful marital relationships take a whole different level of work, work that cannot be charted or graphed. Love is a different creation all in itself. I was still so young and green at the time I was

24 years old and I thought I was king of the world. I just hadn't realized it was just my world inside the four walls of the pizza shop that I ruled. Life teaches us lessons; the universe chooses when those lessons will be learned.

I was granted two wonderful and now healthy boys, both grown and both in college. One who chose to pursue his goal of becoming a lawyer, I hope he makes it. But for any reason if he falls short of his lofty goal his choice will deliver him a quality education. His goal is driven by the broken Justice system that caused me to be writing this book from the Camden County Jail, in New Jersey.

Much of my ability developing the Instructional DVD program was derived from the failed marriage of my youth. Understanding the emotional needs of a woman was delivered to me some years after my divorce. I learned the value of open communications in the daily relationship as well as in the bedroom. Sharing some of these lessons is just one of the many reasons I developed my DVD program. The simple act of using my instructional video as a couple will surely create an open line of communication. That in turn advances a strong and healthy relationship. One of my tangible goals for the DVD that was 100% achieved in its development, was opening a line to communication. Again, out of my adverse situations came advancement.

The end of my successful pizza years came in 2007 which was also due to a goal. Though it was not one of my own, but of the father of the girl I was dating after my marriage. When her father Howard Boehm realized that his daughter Michele and I had young love, it scared the heck out of him. 'Daddy's little girl syndrome', I believed it would pass as time went by. Within a few years I realized I was wrong!

Howard, felt this way because I was divorced, had two young children and a business; he believed that his little girl would be fourth on my priority list. To him this was not acceptable, by our third or fourth date this became apparent to me. He took me aside and informed me in no uncertain terms saying, "I promise I will use all of my financial might to bring you down, when this ends." Howard was patient as goals often require. He likely did not write out the goal. But, I would bet he spoke it aloud in front of the mirror many times over the seven years we dated.

At some point in the first two years Michele proposed marriage to me, taking me to a very romantic location and gave me a romantic card and a ring. I felt happy and grateful that she had such deep feelings for me. We for purposes of pretense and being 'politically correct' at the time got a ring for her as well. It was a cubic zirconium set in gold because we were not prepared to spend the money needed for a diamond. We were fine with this. She went to announce this to her parents, keeping in mind she was twenty five at the time, and the one who actually proposed.

Howard became livid. Michele's dad and I rarely spoke even when at family events together, we kept our distance. He became enraged that his permission was not asked. His anger festered. It was sometime after the new millennium, I was never informed of his rage until a year or so later in a heated argument. Howard further grew his desire to "bring me down." This made his plan backed by the 5th step in goal setting, combine a *deep passion behind your goal to 'make it'* happen. Howard again bided his time waiting for the prime moment to execute his original plan. When we think passionately on something long enough we magnetize what is needed to accomplish our goals.

Michele and I finally had a heated argument about the pizza business. I poured luke-warm coffee down her back with the sole intent of soaking her underwear so she would have to leave the pizza store thus defusing the argument. She being more physical than me punched me in the face in anger. Howard pounced, now was his time.

The original argument was over repayment of her $20,000 investment in the business. She was being offered $50,000 by an outside party. She really didn't want to leave me or be bought out. She had grown attached to the business even though we had ended the relationship a year earlier mostly due to stresses between her dad and me. Michele always said, "He will be dead by 55, like the other men in his family and we'll be fine." I assured her, he would hang in there if only to somehow use *his financial might* against me. Well, I turned out to be correct. Passion can drive a person far beyond any genetic disposition of health.

The simple idea of a *FATHER*, with a passionate love for his only daughter, regardless of how evil based, was enough to keep him alive and awaiting the chance to exact his power and wrath. However, as with most evil or negatively directed goals, he had to cheat. Telling the truth was not an option because there is no winning this evil based goal without a level of deception involved. He caused his wonderfully honest to a fault daughter Michele Boehm to perjure herself in multiple legal documents, sworn affidavits and her testimony on the stand at trial in the Camden County Superior Court.

I delayed the publishing of this text to wait for the statute of limitations to expire, again to protect Michele. The fact is I know she straight out lied, though truly she was never guilty of perjury, due to the duress and coercion of her father; even though she could have stood up and told the truth. Her dad's ongoing threat to tell her, "You'll never see your mother again." Meaning that Michele, would not be welcome in her father's house and be disowned.

Howard's passion for the accomplishment of this goal was so strong he attracted all the corruption he needed to get his task done. With the use of all of his financial might he hired a dishonest lawyer, **Cynthia Levin of the firm Gerstein Grayson in Haddonfield, New Jersey** to prepare untrue on face value civil documents and violated her oath as an officer of the court.

The magnetism of Howard's goal along with the assistance of a dishonest lawyer, Cynthia Levin esq, called the aid of unknowing Collingswood Police Department as well as the misconduct of the **Camden County Prosecutors Office.**

Then **Judge Thomas A. Brown Jr., JSC - Camden County Superior Court Presiding Criminal Judge,** was so attracted to Howard's goal that he, in my opinion, never read the law and simply assumed that I must have been guilty. Assuming the prosecutor knew his job and I must have been criminal in what I was attempting. My virtuous goal was to keep Michele, who I loved very much, safe. She told the truth to the Honorable Judge Stephen Holden in Family Court and his Ruling was against her, dismissing the applications for a Restraining Order, and admonishing Michele for assaulting me. I never broke the criminal code in any way. I even attempted to fire my attorney at the conclusion of the lost trial, because he had admitted to the Judge that he was on pain medication causing him to not submit pre-trial motions or show up for the first pre-trial hearing. Judge Brown would not allow this termination.

There are three purposes for the preceding four pages. First to show that a goal once set, and mixed with step 5 the passion and patience will almost always attract what is needed for its accomplishment; whether it is a positive or negative goal. Second because as this book gains popularity people will investigate my background and start to question my virtue. I want to be forthcoming and inform the public of my behavior as well as the truth surrounding my wrongful incarceration. Third so everyone reading understands that they too can overcome obstacles. Had these things never happened to me over the past six years I would likely not be writing this text, and certainly not from Camden County Jail in my cell in the 3 North A wing on 2/15/2012. Life has very strange twists and turns yet if you stay honest with the world and yourself and stay on course of "Your Mind's Eye" it is very likely you will magnetize all the things needed to do anything you put your mind to. Goals just make it easy to chart and stay on track!

P.S. Most recently with the use of goals posted in my cell I was able to magnetize $3000.00 in investment money I needed to promote, THE BIG SOAK INSTRUCTIONAL DVD and for the publishing and promotion of this book.

"The truth has a way of coming out, but it takes time!"
Valerie Taylor, Eastern Regional High School

"People are just as happy as they make up their minds to be." — Abraham Lincoln

"Success is going from failure to failure without losing your enthusiasm." — Abraham Lincoln

Adversity Brings Improvements

Without my arrival in jail I would likely not be writing this book at all. I say this because once in the housing area where I now live, odd chance brought me to my first cellmate Anthony Johnson in 71 up of the 3 North A wing. After sharing stories the first night after lock-in @ 11 PM, I told him I was in the middle of writing a book on my father and my hospital stay in Boston and New York. He leaned under his bed to pull out a clear 55 gallon trash bag. Inside this bag was a single book, it was titled 'DAN POYNTER'S GUIDE TO SELF-PUBLISHING 7TH EDITION'. The chances of this single book in this single cell would be slim had it not actually happened to me. I love non-fiction and was in dire need to read something other than the romance novel I was given in '7 day', oh, and the Susan Powder Book, which was not bad......

7 Day - The area of the jail where new prisoners are quarantined until they have cleared their hepatitis testing.

I hoped that reading this book would pass the time and perhaps give me some insight on what to do with my book 'THE CAREGIVERS GUIDE TO SANITY – Health Care Proxy' that I was in the midst of writing prior to my coming to jail.

In my mind this was not a chance encounter. It was written in the cards. I wrote out my 16 Week Goals which corresponded to my expected release date. At the top of the page I jotted a statement – "God is in control here 100% and I have just been along for the ride." What I mean by this is everything that brought me to this point and to this place was beyond my ability to control. Even Howard Boehm and his coercion of his daughter Michele may have been prewritten to bring me 'in hindsight' to this point in my life. Since I was young I have consistently <u>self-programmed</u> to be receptive to the things around me that were positive. Always trying to find the positive, in any given situation, no matter how small and not dwell on the negative. In life when handed lemons it was commonplace for me to make lemonade, which is not difficult if you know how. The entire 'HOW & WHY' in my life has brought me to now! I cannot believe that all these things are just coinciding chance happenings. I am 100% convinced that the pathway for the remainder of my life will be to mentor in some way or another. Though writing this text and the production of the DVD will just be a step off location for this trek. I have had so many goals that without the proper awareness and recognition would never have gotten off the drawing board. The Big Soak DVD is good and all, but without this text it is one of many in the marketplace to choose from. Bringing the written word of 'What Lead Me Here' lets me step out of the Internet realm and into book stores eventually. With my previous experience publishing and printing, I think self-publishing will allow my foundation to retain 100% of the profits rather than a small percentage that a New York publisher would offer. This is one of the many ways I see to make lemonade from the lemons in my world.

Development of the DVD surely had its obstacles. Using cutting edge software for most people is as scary as anything in life. Change is something most people don't want to approach. For me it was always something new to understand and learn from, which I love. Without all of the random events in my life and constantly embracing change I would never have had the self-confidence to take the task at hand and look at it as accomplishable.

There were a number of challenges, with the how. The first was how to record quality video, moving quickly into the HD market. My answers came from a customer at the pizza place. A videographer customer Mike, who had shot my television commercial for airing on Comcast years earlier, came into Echo to order wings on a late afternoon in 2006. I inquired what it would cost me to have his company shoot a 30 minute sex-education video.

Thankfully Mike's level of respect for me allowed him to not be selfish and instead be honest, catching me up on new technology. He told me about the problems that he was encountering while filming with top quality analog equipment. He explained that in the new world of digital, even his company with top skills and equipment was having problems with conversion from tape to digital. They had recently purchased an inexpensive amateur camcorder that uses a Mini-DV system. He went on to explain what they have been doing is using the high quality equipment and lenses and then running the analog video through the Mini-DV camera to have the output needed in this now digital world.

Mike let me know that for under $500.00 I would be able to purchase a Mini-DV camcorder as well as the lighting needed to film the entire project myself in the privacy of my home. I was amazed. I would never have been able to complete The Big Soak project on such a low budget, without the assistance of Mike. Just one more reason that my previous endeavors, in this case a failed Chicken & Ribs Restaurant which I had boldly advertised on television, would help my future in some unseen way.

The second challenge of producing your own video production is after the shoot itself. I did not have the next questions prepared by the time Mike's wings were done. It was now up to me to be a bit resourceful.

I remembered back to my Internet years using the computer wiz kids I had known then. I attempted first to consult each of them, yet they were too involved with other projects and my software guru was unreachable. One of them however told of a program made by Adobe, called Premiere-Pro. This is video editing software which is of a far better standard than the Windows Movie Maker that was bundled with the current version of Windows XP.

An employee Paul once told me of a family member of his who was a computer wiz. Being inexperienced with the new software I purchased I contacted Billy, the cousin of Paul, my employee. I made him an offer to be involved in the project if he had the ability to instruct me on the use of the Adobe software.

He was able and willing to participate as most men would have been. I showed him the process I was teaching, and he was happy to learn as well as film the video of me teaching the girls. I was familiar with Adobe software products from my web design days. I used Go Live to construct websites as well as the Photoshop to edit and create artwork. I had also used PageMaker to do the layouts for my restaurants. So for me the learning curve was fairly short.

Once again there is no way I could have done this without the various adversities leading me on a path laid out for me and not really what would have been my first choices. Yet each time these paths financially sustained my life and kept me honest and true to my goals.

As I had predicted to Michele on the 22nd of February 2006, the pizza store came crashing down around me in 2007, due to the passionate and driven 'Goal' of Howard and Michele Boehm. And my project was stopped in its tracks due to being found guilty at trial. Though this trial was revolting in its conduct and verdict I entered jail with a positive attitude and started writing on the subject matter while putting the video on hold. I was carried through these adverse situations with the close support of family and friends, Lea and the boys. My short incarceration after Michele's perjury and Judge Brown's negligence of the law allowed me to survey hundreds of men in the attempt to write a book on female ejaculation instruction.

Once reading the text after my release, it was not easy to understand as I would have hoped. So, my goal drove me back to the video. I now had time on my hands to actually produce the video which we now speak of. Being able to do this because I was out of the pizza business is likely why I pursued this project with passionate vigor at that time. I needed more footage which meant a couple more volunteers.

I started paying close attention to my original goal. The daily affirmation allowed for magnetization to my ideas. I started advertising on Craigslist and got mostly replies from men who were pimping women. This was not at all what I wanted! I was looking for women who truly had a desire to learn how to ejaculate and were willing to have their mid-sections filmed.

One more time the hands of *'Goal Magnetization'* played its role. While at probation I ran into a girl I knew only as a customer of Echo, she had fallen on hard times and in dire need of help. I allowed her to

113

move in with my son Max and me because she was homeless. She and I were not intimate, I was abstaining from relations at the time because there already was far too much turmoil in my life and my only priority was my son staying safe. My other son was safe living with his mother and step-father. Max was sent to me because of headstrong 15 year old behaviors. I was thrilled to have him, ☺. Over the 2 months she was with us, I was working on editing the video I had already filmed. She inquired what it was all about.

Once she realized what my project was about and what it was I was trying to accomplish with it when completed, she wanted to help me in return. I explained the process and she told me it was unlikely that she would be able to ejaculate. Her ex-husband and she were very sexual and she told me she was very orgasmic.

She knew what I was talking about regarding the g-spot and a g-spot orgasm, in her mind. She was one that was comfortable with masturbation; this was an area where my production was lacking. Her willingness to allow me to film her was evidence of the attraction when we focus on goals. Even if the instruction I would give her did not yield the resulting female ejaculation I would still be able to use the video footage to demonstrate the movements to later describe the actions in my narration.

We had filmed all night with Billy on the camcorder and another girl that had already worked with me. My housemate was able to witness how the process worked because girl #2 had already filmed with me and was able to come to a full ejaculating orgasm during this shoot. She had even revealed to me that she could now achieve this herself through masturbation but was not willing to be filmed doing so. These explanations helped to put my housemate at ease. She was able to gain an understanding.

There were little results from my first attempt to get the new to girl to learn to ejaculate, though she did get through it with the feelings that she need to urinate, which is the first step. After some sleep she woke and started masturbation I asked if she could go pee first and if I could start filming, she agreed. She had gotten herself all worked up, following my directions, but again no marked results. At that point I stepped in and took over. Her being sexually worked up allowed me to come into frame and she now already had an idea from the previous night how it would feel. In this instance I was able to create the most amazing orgasm she had ever experienced as well as bring her to full ejaculation. This is the girl who is facing down in the instructional video with the convulsing vagina, as well as the masturbation demonstration segment.

Iconoclast
"i-con-o-clast"

Iconoclast - a person who attacks cherished beliefs, traditional institutions, etc., as being based on error or superstition. Though, it also refers to destruction of religious Icons which does not apply to me in this case.

Opinions are swiftly changing to understand that female ejaculation is not urine, and it is a genuine sexual function of the human body. The public at large is still very Victorian-traditional in their ideas about sex and women. The younger audience has become more educated and realistic towards the realities of sex mostly due to the excessive amount of pornography as well as educational video on the Internet. Today 2/27/2012 there are now categories within most pornographic directories for *squirters*, which has only occurred in the last two years or so. My goal would be that these categories by 2015 to change titles to 'female ejaculation' or 'orgasmic expulsion' with the aid of this text. Yet at this point calling it squirting is the common expression in the non-scientific community, but taken by some as glorifying the pornographic content of female ejaculation. This somewhat concentrates on the action rather than the natural process by not using the proper defining words. With regard to the male, these sites use terms as 'big ejaculators' not slangs.

Whether the final term becomes 'Female Ejaculation' which is accepted in the scientific community and Wiki; or what was the public's largest search query as determined by the Google Pull-down 'Female Ejaculatory Discharge' from its onset in 2009 until March 14th of 2010, when the search terms for unknown reasons were deemed pornographic and banned by Google; coinciding with the Australian movie ban on small breasts and female ejaculation in adult films. I was shocked that a scientifically supported sexual reaction be eliminated in world search because of one countries diminished views.

118

A universally standard term needs to be put in place. I have written in the past the name Orgasmic Expulsion should be considered being it is the terms used in the original studies by Whipple and Perry in 1980, also why I chose the title for the book. There needs to be a more widespread understanding. Even I am guilty using the 'Squirt' expression do to the need for marketing and search engine placement over the past five years. Hopefully this book will allow me to be known as Eric Jackson and not The Squirt Doctor.

I first shared my video production with Dr. Beverly Whipple, the current authority on the subject of Female Ejaculation in 2009 when through some strange twist of fate I Googled myself and found that she lived about a mile from me, in Southern New Jersey. So I contacted her and requested her expert opinion. Afterward she informed me that she was not able to endorse the DVD because of one single reason: it's *GOAL* oriented. I promote the realities of my experience. I am confident that that process is not exclusive to just some women. I have been able to facilitate first time expulsion experiences repeatedly because I know what I am doing and communicate with the woman. Sexual behaviors are like any other behavior, they are learned from experience. The singular reason Dr. Whipple supports my efforts is because I do my best to try to spread the word and the information I share actually covers the natural processes.

As far as I am concerned what can be learned by one person can be taught to another. It is all in the communication, whether the teacher explained that communication in the relationship is key to the ejaculation process working. This is providing that no handicap exists. In this case of Orgasmic Expulsion the handicap would be more likely to have to be physical rather than mental.

Since 2005 when I started the conversation about this subject, I was not alone in the iconoclast movement to break the taboo and social mores surrounding female ejaculation. Hopefully this text will further the efforts.

In 2006 the Internet which is one of my fortes offered little help on the subject. As I have said we had Wikipedia just starting to become popular because of their top ranking within the search engines like Yahoo and Google. But still there was little information from the general public who had the skills to contribute to this forum. And the experts of the time on female ejaculation did not have the skills needed or desire to employ a computer geek to submit their expert opinions to the public via Wiki. Contributions from people like me who were Internet savvy would not consider ourselves expert enough to do more than add a line here and there or delete information known to be completely inaccurate. Slowly over the next several years Wiki became the site that received top SEO ranking because of the vast amount of data it offered on almost every subject. This is how and why SEO is a science all on its own, which will be discussed in the chapter on Google Ranking.

SEO - Search Engine Optimization - The coding used in a webpage allowing it to correctly be sorted by a search engine with hopes of top ten ranking.

Of the last half century since the onset of mass media the greatest sexual iconoclasm was without a doubt The G-Spot book in 1982 by Alice Kahn Ladas M.M.S.,Ed.D., Beverly Whipple, PH. D., and John Perry, PH. D. That publication single handedly changed sex talk forever (I am reading it now in April 2012).

The impact was so timely rolling into the new decade, leaving the care-free 70's with something to be desired. When the 'G-spot' was talked about on television it was a first, but by no means going to be ignored by the new era of broadcasters coming on the scene trying to capture the Neilson Ratings of the day. It was almost as strong a wave as the onset of the Internet at the end of the 90's. Sex sells, period. To all of a sudden be able to now talk about it on TV and cover the book written by noted medical professionals within their community was a big win for broadcasters as well as the authors. The general public eventually became the true winner.

It opened a new line when communicating about sex. It quickly became a topic of coffee table talk and a great bar conversation between friends nationwide. By the time I finished High School in 1984 everyone knew about and was searching out the G-spot.

Perhaps the simple X marks the spot search was part of the problem. In this western society that is on a constant search for the next, best thing, it may have been too much factual information without evolutionary education to back it up. The majority of people looking for the G-spot within the vaginal cavity never read the book. Nor had a basic anatomy education to understand, the information being disseminated from person to person.

In 2007 when I was first wrongly held in jail for a trial verdict which was just outright wrong, I used my time to survey over 250 men I came in contact with over the eight weeks prior to being paroled.

Taking into consideration that many inmates statistically have lower IQ and are less exposed to literature, these men are seemingly as well informed on sexual relations as any professionals I have spoken with.

-My first question is usually, "Have you heard of the G-spot?" Almost all agreed they had.

-Second, "Where is it?" 50% believe it is the clitoris, which of course was stated with varying levels of slang. 10% confused it with the body's erogenous zones, neck, ears, knees, etc. The 40% that knew it was inside the vaginal cavity gave varying answers to its location. But all of them considered it to be a pea or dime sized little button that needs to be pressed. Not a single one had ever heard of Dr. Whipple or the book that made the term G-SPOT famous. Only 1 in 5 admitted, ever having had a woman soak the sheet and only half those men knew why it happened or what caused it.

Current day, 2012 I am back in county jail. I failed to complete my five years of probation because after four successful years I ditched to help two dying men, my best friends' dad and my own father. I am writing this page a week before my 80th day in jail, I will be released in about 9 days. My new surveys revealed significant changes in opinions. Yes all have heard of the G-spot, but now almost 70% of men surveyed are aware of the come here motion is something needed to get a reaction from the spot. And now over 75% also know it is inside the vagina. I must mention that statistically there are now 25% more men under the age of 23 than there were in 2007 and most of them have gained their knowledge via the Internet and a few revealed that HBO's REAL SEX was the source of their education on this subject.

So at this point in history media and 'new media' seem to be an astounding source of education. Now almost all the under 30 crowd claims to all have had women soak the sheets to varying degrees, due to orgasmic expulsion not just vaginal secretions, some through manual stimulation inside the vagina and some through clitoral stimulation, very few from intercourse. This time the pool was just short of 300 men ages 19 to 52. These drastic changes in five short years are overwhelming and inspiring to me as an instructor and expert in the subject.

Yet with websites like my own, Wikipedia, Yahoo Answers and Dr. G out there providing free information to anyone who logs on, has literally changed the world as far as female ejaculation goes. So in the new millennium the Internet itself and its expert contributors have become the current sexual iconoclasm. The information out there and my website statistics from You Tube show the largest searching audience is women ages 45 to 65 by an overwhelming percentage. Because of the freedom of individuals like me and others to post freely information is abundant. People in the world are now smart enough to vet the information by backing it up from multiple sources.

Why I am Writing This Book in Jail

Well the simplest answer I can give to the why of this text, is the desire to leave a record. The statement <u>The Pen Is Mightier than the Sword</u> came about for a reason. Once something is put in ink it tends to leave a completely different mark on society as a whole. The DVD is a wonderful tool, and something that is somewhat timeless in its own right, but once pen hits paper, like with goals things change.

Next, without a doubt, it has swiftly passed my now eight weeks in jail for violation of probation, the offence I did plead guilty to, because I was. I knew putting my father's life above my freedom, no matter what the price I would pay later, was worth every risk! At this point my father's days are still numbered but every day for the most part is decent quality of living with some more to accomplish. Letting him die in September of 2011 because the doctors would not do anything but pain management seemed unthinkable to me. So crossing multiple state lines and skipping out on probation as bad an idea as it was, it made sense to me.

As I am writing I am starting to think for this to be a true autobiography, I really owe it to the public to convey some of what goes on in jail. I write these pages from here, so why not convey a little bit about life inside the walls.

At this point I have all my goals on the walls of my cell, as I exit every time I am reminded of them. Writing also keeps me in my cell while all the turmoil takes place in what I call the 'playground'.

> Playground – The main hall of housing areas in a jail.

Writing keeps me grounded in the realities of the business and outside world which I live. The 'kampers' in here are jail professionals. Many of them have more pleasure in here, than in the outside world.

> Kampers - The term I feel should be assigned instead of inmates or offenders, because the Jail System really offers no correction it is just a sleep away camp for adults.

I am not prepared to take part in that type of thinking. It takes daily efforts to not fall in with the rest of the nonsense that goes on in here. Not to say everything is bad but almost everything runs in the circles of acting tuff. Most times in life we tend to start thinking and acting like those we expose ourselves to most. *There is currently screaming outside my door about why someone's partner in spades (the card game) threw out diamonds first.*

They are literally screaming over something so stupid. Keeping my door closed and working at my desk leads me to keep some level of sanity. For the reality it could be the New York Stock Exchange yelling outside my door and most times I completely ignore the content. The commotion is to the same level. The yelling in every movie we have ever seen involving Wall Street is what I witness on a daily basis here in jail, yet it is never for the greater good. All the exchange here is for exhibition of personal power that lasts all of about five minutes.

Let me share what most law abiding citizens in American don't know about jail. Jail is not Prison! Prison is what is seen on the reality television shows and in movies. Both have their many codes, but in Prison the violations of those codes comes with punishment which include and are not limited to getting killed at lunch. Jail is a temporary housing area for short term kampers. People without the ability to make bail, or held without bail awaiting trial, and those awaiting the transfer to prison.

Jail is no more or less than your standard sleep away camp for grown-ups, hence why I address the inmates as kampers. Don't get me wrong there is some level of posturing for power and there are fights. Yet from what I have observed the majority of the guards here keep the order to some degree; yet many are just as big a part of the problem letting the non-sense go on.

As with everything there are a couple of bad apples in every bunch, guards that are power mongers, taking advantage of their authority position to intimidate prisoners. Sgt. G. Snapp and his team of goons, C.O. Lovel and C.O. Rhodes, between the three of them my life was threatened on more than one occasion; though, I must give C.O. Rhodes credit for preventing C.O. Lovel from physically attacking me late one night. Thankfully there are also guards that take protecting prisoners seriously, C.O. Crossan, C.O. Kale, C.O. Swain, C.O. Boardley are among the few and those that kept me safe in various situations. This story will be expanded in my future title "90 DAYS AROUND THE JAIL."

There are basic rules in here, but beyond that it is mostly a run wild environment where as long as there is no physical violence most things are left to the kampers to iron out. Sometimes when there is a physical act, the guards just stand by and watch as long as it is only a fist fight. I see no weapons as it goes, shy of the pen in my hand. There are little reasons to take the risk of a possibly short term stay versus extending it due to causing someone physical injury and getting a new charge. There are rules in jail and **Fist beats Sword, but the Pen is mightier than the Fist,** in here. A well written grievance or complaint causes problems for all involved, Corrections Officers and kampers, equally.

There is what's called shakedowns; this is where mass groups of guards storm the housing area. They pull everyone out of their cells provided they are not already out. Strip you down to your underwear and search your entire cell from top to bottom. For the most part they come across extra towels and blankets that the kampers are hoarding without medical reasons. But sometimes they come across drugs both prescription and street substances and cigarettes. As well they remove all and any decoration from cell walls which are secured with tooth paste and water removable; cloth lines for drying underwear, socks, towels and sheets; and some other inventive things that can be made with thread, and plastic spoons. Those on the inside of the walls call this *JAILIN*. Though these items are all against the rules, they are the little bits of creativity needed to live life in jail. I find it funny that the same guards doing the shakedown walk in our cells on a daily basis and never mention a word about the walls or the cloth lines.

There are your standard clicks here. In here however most of the time it is a keep to your own gang association, religion, and race in that order. Then there are the few outsiders like myself that don't fit in at all and it is very obvious. First my skin is white, though I am only half white from my mother's side; my father is mixed half black and half Portuguese. But even though it is 2012 people still only see skin color, sad but true. So being raised by a Jewish mom and a large Jewish extended family I see things in a completely different light versus most of the men in here which are 50% black and 30% Latin as I observe it. *2-23-12 - The kampers are all quiet. Their snack orders just came in. The room went from one of the loudest nights I have heard to date, to almost somber. As all the kampers count their Raman Noodles, Cookies and Coffee, making careful accounting not to be missing a cheese sauce or candy bar, or they would raise hell to the Corrections Officers, if one item was shorted.*

My Theory of
Female Ejaculate Fluids

Most of us have a basic scientific understanding of the human body from our primary education of biology. We know that there are many systems within the human body. Those include but are not limited to the muscular system, skeletal, urinary, nervous, dermal (skin), digestive, and circulatory system. In addition to the circulatory system which is responsible for about half of the fluid transport of the body, the half which involves red blood cells and their connection to gas transfer (oxygen and carbon dioxide) as well as nutrient and waste transfer from our cells. The other half of the fluid transport in the human body is moved in what is called lymphatic system. Lymph fluid is most similar in chemical make up to the interstitial fluids (the between) that fill our blood stream called plasma or serum. This is largely made up of water.

Interstitial fluid is also the fluid that surrounds all the cells of our bodies, actually bathing the cells.

We hear that we are made up of mostly water. We can now begin to understand where this water is hanging out inside us, in and around our cells, in our lymph and in the serum that allows the blood and waste to travel in our circulatory system.

Our lymphatic system is connected to the glands in our bodies. Glands are separated in two categories. Exocrine and endocrine as the names sort of communicate their individual function. The root meaning of endo is *within*, while exo is *outside of*. Endocrine glands are those like in our neck that swell when we are sick. While exocrine glands, are like our sweat glands and breast glands which leak out.

The medical profession has been long confused about the glands in the vagina. Let us think in simple terms, men are formed from women at around week six in the fetal stage. That said, the penis must form from something? The Y chromosome instructs our external development to take place. Where do these parts come from? My logic is they are the parts transformed from our female counterparts. I believe that if we break it down all the parts are the same, just located in different areas. The head of the male penis

136

and foreskin is the same part as the clitoris and clitoral hood (glans). The urethra is located just below the clitoris. The labia minora (inner lips) in my opinion transforms to become the shaft of the penis, while the labia majora (outer lips) transform to become the male scrotum.

We hear stories where boys only have one testicle descend... this leads me to believe that my testis are truly transformed ovary. If you can understand what I have just described then where are the rest of the parts that cause erection and ejaculation. I am confident that they're still in there. The prostate gland is responsible for the fluid that is in male ejaculate as well as anal excretions (milking the prostate). The majority of the old millennium medical profession is not up to speed on the fact that women have the same prostate gland as men. I have even been told by Dr. Broncado the puppet psychiatrist in the Camden County Jail that I was truly insane if I believed that women had a prostate gland. Yet since the mid 1980's the organization that standardizes the name of anatomical parts has called the urethral sponge the female prostate gland.

The prostate is an exocrine gland. My theory is that the prostate gland located anterior (towards the belly button) to the inside wall of the vagina is in union with the other glandular tissues. These other tissues become the base of the male penis, including the wings of the clitoris which extend to the interior of the vagina. The Y chromosome causes the male prostate to migrate further up the urethra beyond the base of the penis near the anus, for its proper function. These tissues are located inside the vagina surrounding the urethra, running towards the belly button. This area when stimulated with the correct pressures and friction engorge with fluid in a woman.

We understand without need of proof that if you burn your skin... you suddenly get a blister... where did that water come from so quickly? It is the interstitial fluids of the body, the fluid that surrounds the cells, and flows in the blood stream, as well as the lymphatic system. There is an abundant amount fluid in our bodies. Under the right circumstances these fluids flow to the needed areas freely and extremely swiftly.

I theorize that the mild irritation of the tissues of the upper abdominal wall of the inner vagina causes excretions to flush through the urethra as a cleansing reflex. These excretions are not urine in their makeup which is a waste product produced slowly through the kidneys. The rush of what I believe to be the interstitial fluids of the entire body flow gushingly with the muscle spasmodic behaviors of orgasm, it is because of the rhythm of muscles contracting in our bodies that move our lymphatic system also keeping control of heavy rhythmic breathing. The bladder and kidneys are fluid rich organs; the glands in the G-Area are all fluid rich glands and direct outlets for the lymphatic system. Put down a towel because this level of release is truly abundant and pleasurable.

When I finished editing I found empty pages to account for new chapters starting on odd pages. I figure I would use this space to deliver some unrelated wisdom.

I am not one for giving stock tips other than to family, but if you have read this far in my book you deserve to know what I know in whole. (frbk) symbol on the stock exchange is a bank. There is one in Haddonfield, NJ down the block from where I live. It is being run by many of the former executives of Commerce Bank which started in South Jersey and was sold out to TD Bank of Canada. The Moment I Walked In, I Felt Like I Was Home! Feels like coming home!

Banking is an important part of our lives and this is a young company that is growing in the direction that I watched Commerce Bank grow first hand in the market where I do all of my business. It may be worth a look! At around $2.00 a share you may want to trust me, you may not....

How I Got Top Rank
On Google

Many years ago when the Internet was in its 1.0 stage: search engines used people to do much of their organizing. The Open Directory (aka DMOZ) was one of the larger of the user submitted directories. The benefit of these types of search listings were that once you were a recognized contributor, your sites tended to receive better ranking. There were many sites to submit your URL and hope you were early enough in your category that you were seen. This is when there were only thousands of sties listed for a category not hundreds of thousands or millions as we see in the Internet 3.0.

We now depend more on the robots and spiders of the Google algorithms to define our life or death visibility in the user search world. It is beneficial to submit to as many other sites in your industry as possible because of the strength of cross linking which has remained very hot. The more places that links to your site are seen on the net the better potential ranking you will receive by the larger search engines like Google and Yahoo.

Now in the time of the current 'Internet 3.0' (the newest generation with social networking) there is more significance to the location of your 'cross link' (other sites where your URL is listed). Google utilizes an algorithm, which is a very sophisticated string of mathematical probability equation; this is used by their system to determine the likelihood of a user that is typing in search terms - gets the listings that they are actually looking for and most helpful. Crosslinks are now gauged based on the Page Ranking of the site your link appears. Page Ranking or PR value is the value given by Google to a page with regard to its own worth and usefulness. Cross linking on these pages is not an item that you can overlook in today's market of search ranking. Being listed on a page like Wikipedia gives you a better chance of getting higher ranking on

Google because Wiki is a reliable site when compared to others it has a PR of 10. Other pages like WordPress and other top quality blogs, as well as sites like E-Bay all attain top PR values as you can see when you search the net yourself. So if you are able to find a category within these sites that applies to your product or service you need to sign up as a member and then learn to edit the page to include your information and external link as a source of more information on the subject.

There is also a 'trick' if you have a public interest topic within your website you should offer links to other sites (resources page links) like the .gov locations that offer official information relating to your subject. The more links the better. I have a lawyer site that I developed at the end of the 90's that offers every governmental organization in the book. He has maintained top ranking for the past 10 years because his site is an actual resource for the user. So consider a useful links page within your site.

Since 2009 when Google began the pull down bar, where the computer knows what you are thinking before you finish typing, SEO designers were given the best clue of all, literally given the answers to the key question! What are users searching, and what keywords do they type in their search query. This was the gold mine of search information for owners of web sites. Many site owners could not take advantage of this information because they were not in charge of development of their own sites.

Realizing this, you must be involved and take some control of the search engine optimization of your own site. You know your product and the customers that you are looking to acquire. Your contribution in the assistance of your web designer and search engine ranking team is important, perhaps the most important of all. There are niche areas that the web developers are not aware of because they are not in your industry. You need to do the homework as I did. Keep searching for your own site, even if you must go 10 or 20 pages deep to find yourself. Ask yourself the questions I used.

1. Identify what is the product or service that makes money from my website?
2. How would I search for this product or service if looking for my competition?
3. How do I separate myself from them within the search criteria, stand out from the crowd?
4. Is there an area that I can identify where my product or service can be seen in a search area

the other top ranked sites are missing or lacking?

5. What are the keywords of the top ranked sites in my category? To find this information go to the top ranking site of your choice and right click or find the dropdown that contains the words "view page source" this will bring you to the html scripting contained within the page, in a separate window that looks like code. Within the top few lines of this code you will find something called META – this information is the data that is used by the search engine spiders and robots (a name given to the virus like information finders that do not damage your site but look for the content so the search engines can sort it properly). Spiders or robots will enter your site and only look at the code which causes the page to appear to your user as it does. The developer of your site may or may not have included "keyword" META tags within your sites coding as well as unique page title META tags. Unique page titles also improve rank when they include keywords.

6. What is in their META tags? Copy from other top ranked sites!

7. How can I include these tag keywords in my site?

For me, my site is in the category of sex. Now we all know the strongest Internet searches relate to sex are related to the pornographic websites. So the question that stood out on the above list was: *how will I stand out from the crowd?* Realizing at the very beginning I did not want to be categorized within the pornographic categories. Cross linking within the porn sites may have allowed me to achieve better ranking because of their visibility. But I refused to link to any of the pornographic sites because to me it was devaluing my product and concept of instruction. At that moment in 2008 I figured out what my isolation on the Internet would be - INSTRUCTIONAL DVD. I understood the only customer I could look to find were individuals that wished to learn what they had already done some level of research on. As a motorist examines consumer reports on cars, Internet users that wanted to learn about the subject of female ejaculation would likely be educated consumers. I shot for top ranking in the categories of 'squirting instructional dvd' or 'female ejaculation instruction' or 'learn to' and I went to work on my own coding issues. My site was built completely of images and flash animations so it needed to change. My META Tags were in place yet I was not seeing much ranking. I realized I had made a critical error in the way the new search engine algorithms were operating. They still ran on spiders and tagging, yet we were not submitting the sites ourselves like I had with then Internet when I was doing it full time and it had been almost eight years later. The search engine Google's best practices are the basis for all others. If you have top rank on Google then the other search sites giving Google a PR of 10 also ranked your page on top. So to be seen elsewhere on the net in search ranking you are a shoe in if you have top Google ranking.

I completely revamped my site from a beautiful graphic site to a basic text based page of information only and very specific words to make up the landing/home page. I immediately in 2009 added the exact words that the Google pull down reflect which was: 'female ejaculatory discharge'. My rank went from second and third page (20-30) to varying from top 2, 3 and 4 just by including this phrase which applied to my product in the text of the html of my index.html coding. This shot me up in the range of 300 to 500 original users to my site per day, from a previous average of about 30 a day.

In March of 2010 Google for some reason felt this to be a subject no longer worth the use of their pull-down menu bar. Female Ejaculatory Discharge which was listed just below FEMA and just above Female Dogs Name one day disappeared. No longer did Google correct the spelling of female ejaculation or give other suggestions; I was puzzled at the very least. I literally lost hundreds of dollars a month overnight. Since I lost that pull-down listing I have taken measures to have my links on many other sites in appropriate locations, expert sites in medical categories, wiki sites, blog sites as well as answers sites. This has helped me continue to maintain an average count of 70 original visitors per day. I have also used subpages of the site for links as landing pages. I have written articles on my subject submitting them to other expert sites and linking any of my answers or feedback with links to my articles which also receive search ranking on their own. These are just a few simple steps I took to keep my website seen in the vast world of cyberspace.

The key to your website is you. You need to be more involved in the direction of your use of the Internet in your daily business thinking. There are so many places to be seen and show off your product or service for potential customers to purchase.

Lastly I suggest to all who have not already done so, join Google Analytics and place the needed code in your site as soon as you finish this chapter.

"IT'S YOUR LIFE
AND YOUR PARTNER'S
YOU OWE IT TO YOURSELF
TO SEARCH FOR THE BEST
IN AND OUT
OF THE BEDROOM!
GOOD LIFE AND GOOD SEX"
©ERIC JACKSON

"IF IT IS TO BE,
IT IS UP TO ME!"
INSPIRED WORDS FROM A CHILDHOOD FRIEND OF
NIKKI MANJI

QUICK ORDER INFORMATION

e-mail questions: info@adechopublishing.com

Book owners will receive 15% off The Big Soak
Instructional DVD anytime they order by going to
www.thebigsoak.org/ purchase.html

To order single copies for friends please use Amazon .com

Follow us on

YouTube

&

Twitter

@phillysexchat

I dedicate this final page of this book to my father, whose days are few, but he held on long enough to see this in print! I wrote it while in jail to express my feelings to him.

<u>TERMINAL LOVE</u>

IF YOU SPEAK THE TRUTH DECLARE YOUR LOVE
IF YOUR HEART IS TRUE LET IT BE KNOWN
TO USE THE WORDS, BEST BE SINCERE
WHEN YOU ARE, THERE IS NO FEAR

WITHOUT A SINGLE WORD YOU SHOW YOUR LOVE
JUST BY WHAT YOU'VE DONE THERE IS NO MISTAKE
YOU GAVE ME FAITH I TRUSTED WITHOUT FEAR
WITHOUT USING THE PHRASE YOUR ACTIONS WERE CLEAR

LIFE HAS BROUGHT US A RADICAL TURN
WITHOUT YOU TO RANT WITH, I WILL HAVE TO LEARN
THIS NEW ROAD I TRAVEL, I HOLD YOU DEAR
IN MY HEART YOU WILL ALWAYS BE HERE

SO BURNED INTO MY MIND I HAVE NO CHOICE
WHEN IT'S QUIET AND STILL I HEAR YOUR VOICE
WHAT YOU HAVE SHARED WITH ME WILL LIVE ON
I WILL MISS YOU MORE WHEN YOU ARE GONE
Dad, you're my Ace of Diamonds

© ERIC JACKSON 3/2/2012 259583
PUBLISHED 8/14/2012

Made in the USA
Columbia, SC
24 May 2024